Making Mo
Penny Shares &
Small Company
Investments

CW00641112

Making Money From Penny Shares & Small Company Investments

Adrian Ball

KOGAN
PAGE

First published in Great Britain in 1989 by Kogan Page Limited, 120
Pentonville Road, London N1 9JN.

Editorial packaging by Redfern Publishing Services.

While every care has been taken to ensure the accuracy of the con-
tents of this work, no responsibility for loss occasioned to any person acting or refraining from action as a result of any statement in it
can be accepted by the author or publisher.

British Library Cataloguing in Publication Data

Ball, Adrian
   Making money from penny shares and small
   company investments
   1. Great Britain. Stocks – shares Investment
   manuals.
   I. Title
   332.6'322

   ISBN 1–85091–825–2
   ISBN 1–85091–826–0 pbk

Printed and bound in Great Britain by Biddles Limited, Guildford,
Surrey

Contents

Acknowledgements

Numerous people have assisted me in the writing of this book and I would like to acknowledge their advice and support. Above all, I wish to express my gratitude to my Fleet Street colleagues, Vera Madan and Annette Lyen, for their diligent research, word processing and checking.

These pages draw upon facts and figures contributed by more than 100 fund managers and analysts. They are too numerous to identify individually, so I ask them to accept this collective thank-you for their invaluable co-operation.

I turned for expert comment on penny shares to John Snowden of *Penny Share Guide*, John Gommes of *Penny Share Focus*, John Spiers of *Best Investment*, John Houlihan of Hoare Govett and John Coyne, a City Editor who became an expert in 'pennies'. Neil Campbell of Stock Beech and Mark Collins of Fidelity were other sources of objective information.

Finally, I wish to express my thanks for the efficient way in which the public relations departments of the Stock Exchange, the Unit Trust Association, and the Association of Investment Trust Companies provided me with essential background information on the workings of their respective organisations.

Adrian Ball
November 1988

Introduction

'Few of us pause for definitions even in our most serious discussions and when we do we are amazed, not that there is so much bitter misunderstanding and acrimony in life, but that there is so little.' The sage quotation comes from Joseph Odell. As anyone buying a book on investment is clearly hoping for a 'serious discussion', let me begin by trying to state my aim and define my terms.

My main aim is to suggest to the private investor that there should be a place in his or her portfolio for investments both in so-called 'penny shares' and in smaller companies generally. Although these categories of equities have taken sharp punishment in the period since the collapse of international stock markets in October 1987, they have traditionally been good for the small investor. With markets likely to gather more strength in 1989, they should be looked at with even closer interest.

Is this a good time to be urging private investors to return to the fray instead of licking their wounds on the sidelines and studying their building society passbooks? I believe it is an excellent time to invest – especially if you have medium to long-term objectives. There were numerous bargains to be had during the latter part of 1988 and a similar situation will probably still apply early in 1989.

A report from Scottish Amicable published with the 'crash' more than a year behind, detailed just how attractively priced equities had become. Urging unit trust investors to get back into the market, Scottish Amicable pointed out that an investor buying UK equities in November 1988 would be getting 57 per cent more in dividends, 77 per cent more in profits, and 53 per cent more in assets than would have been the case had the same shares been acquired in July 1987 at the height of the market. The bargains are likely to be even greater in the categories of investments covered by this book. The 'blue chips' have been through their recovery period and the good times for the more volatile shares lie just ahead of us.

At this point, let me make a mild apology for some of the terms used in these pages. Although we talk freely of 'penny shares', there are not many instances today where an equity can be picked up for just a few pence. Some people therefore define 'pennies' as shares trading for 70p or less, or even those still in double figures (ie less than 100p). I regard 'pennies' as those priced at 50p or less. Many of these are also 'smaller companies' with market capitalisation of less than, say, £10 million or £20 million. But the professionals have a much wider definition of 'smaller companies' and place in this category companies with capitalisations of £50 million and more.

These are, however, still 'minnows' in comparison with the large quoted companies and I believe they offer, and will continue to offer, good opportunities for the private investor. Smaller companies have been out-performing the market in the UK for at least 30 years and there are good reasons why this has been so. Managements of smaller concerns have greater chances to develop and expand their businesses and this can be reflected quite swiftly in the share price. Such executives can be more nimble, aggressive and innovative than the managers of vast corporations who have to pull off deals of ever increasing size to maintain growth.

Away from the big battalions, the ranks of the smaller companies are comparatively under-researched and this is one of the factors which operate in favour of the investor of modest means. Because of the dearth of information on many small companies, good results or a corporate success can cause a substantial movement upwards in the share price. The same thing rarely happens with a large concern where, thanks to detailed studies by analysts, the share price reflects everything known about the company's progress. Good results often have little or no effect on a large company's rating because the market has discounted the profit well beforehand.

The investor going into the market on his or her own account will not build a fortune by sticking to the 'blue chip' equities. The private speculator with some cash which can be placed at risk should consider a judicious mix of 'pennies' and a larger spread of quoted small companies operating in sectors which seem to be particularly relevant. If you do not feel you have the time, talent, or energy to become involved in the necessary research, then you can take the armchair approach of putting your money into small company unit trusts and investment trusts where professionals will do the work for you.

It is all a question of adopting a 'rifle or shotgun' approach. With the former weapon you will be trying to pinpoint individual stocks as targets. When you elect to go into, say, unit trusts you will be making use of a 'shotgun' technique, scattering the shot widely. Each weapon has its good points – everything depends upon how much effort you are going to put into becoming a marksman.

Whichever course you follow, there is much in contemporary Britain that will operate to your advantage. Although brokers are less interested in helping investors of modest means, sources of information are better and easier to tap than hitherto, facilitating a do-it-yourself approach to investment. Within the target companies, there is a stronger entrepreneurial spirit, with managers aware that good performance can produce large and lightly taxed personal earnings. For all the controversy over Government policies, corporate profits are being boosted by strong direction from Whitehall, fewer strikes, bouyant demand, and a relatively firm currency.

Your own resources will determine your decision on the proportion of the mix between 'pennies' (where you are essentially gambling on a recovery or the injection of new management or products) and smaller company shares (where the risk is far less provided you invest in the right niche of the market). Coming towards the end of 1988 both classes seemed to be heading towards brighter trading in 1989, even if the heady heights of July 1987 stay out of reach. Even the most enthusiastic tipsters in the penny share game admit there is not another Polly Peck (9p to £35) on the horizon or a Pentland Industries (20p to £30), but they see the decade coming to an end with a revival in 'pennies' that will bring investors back into the market.

You should be warned that becoming a penny share investor will be a rather lonely business. Newspapers rarely spotlight special opportunities among lowest-priced shares and financial magazines tend to run no more than annual features on the subject. You will have to get into the habit of making your own judgements on the prospects for run-down companies that have little left but their Stock Exchange quote or those performing well which may, or may not, be in a profitable product or service niche.

City professionals tend to shun penny shares as a genre and are not very helpful to small investors seeking advice on them. They often give the impression that there is something faintly rakish, even improper, about the whole business. Although a stockbroker will accept 'executive only' business from a client dealing in any kind of share, a penny share is unlikely to be represented in any list of recommendations. The research departments of most stock-brokers just do not bother about the lower-priced offerings.

I certainly felt like one of the characters of celebrated 1940s cartoonist H M Bateman, when talking about penny shares to some of our leading firms of stockbrokers. I was the little fellow in a bowler hat, carrying an umbrella and made to feel a complete bounder because I uttered the words 'penny shares' within the portals of a great stockbroking house. Around me, airborne in shock and rage, I envisaged a circle of brokers in black jackets and striped trousers.

Laurence Prust & Company said they 'do not welcome penny share dealing'. Rowe and Pitman observed sternly, 'no dealing here in penny shares'. At Warburg Securities the message was 'no dealing at this level'. Kleinwort Benson told me that, if clients were interested, they would be advised to look at unit trusts or invest-ment trusts dealing in smaller companies. Fiske & Company reported 'no analyst for penny shares and no dealing in them'. Shearson Lehman Securities commented tersely, 'no penny stocks, no statistics, do not deal at that level'. An almost identical comment came from another trans-Atlantic house, Chase Manhat-tan Securities. 'We do not really cover penny shares. No research data is available.'

County NatWest (incorporating the old-established firm of Wood Mackenzie & Company) wrote to me to say, 'We do not cover penny shares as a sector and none of the companies we fol-low falls within your definition. I am afraid that we have no statis-tical information which would be useful to you.' De Zoete & Bevan reminded me that penny shares were speculative and that they dealt mainly with the institutions while Green & Company simply did not operate at the 'low end of the scale'. So it is easy to under-stand why I felt like a man in a Bateman cartoon!

A few stockbrokers – most of them smaller firms – said they were willing to trade in penny shares on behalf of private clients. Their names are listed in Chapter 9; but they comprise a small minority of the total roll-call of London and provincial brokers. Why is this? If the experts are so wary of penny shares, should private investors dabble in them at all? The answer is that a dedicated band of investors exists who want a little excitement and the chance of accumulating profits at a higher rate than with conventional investment. Provided the investor is not committing funds needed for the maintenance of a home or family and the amount invested is just a part of a portfolio, then penny shares can yield both profit and pleasure.

Luck and timing can play a large part, but there is also the need for skill and application. It is not like filling in a football coupon. The more you learn about a company, the sector in which it is operating and the general progress of the economy, the more likely you are to be a winner in the penny shares game. It is an intellectual pursuit as well as a calculated gamble. Buying the tipsheets, and keeping your eyes open for newspaper leads, are not the only requirements. You have to become something of an analyst yourself – for this is the great 'do-it-yourself' section of the personal finance world.

This book is aimed at those of you who are interested in investing 'off the beaten track'. It is by no means confined to penny shares and the riskier side of equity investment. On the contrary, the main thrust is in the field of smaller and emerging companies whose share prices may, or may not, be inexpensive at the time of purchase. Not all the smaller companies are penny shares and certainly not all the 'pennies' can be found among the smaller fry – from time to time 'whales' also appear in this particular pool.

I have linked penny shares (which usually carry a high element of risk) with investment in smaller companies (which is a logical, and safer activity) because they are both 'off the beaten track'. Most stockbrokers are terrified of the former and wary, or ignorant, about the latter. For good reasons, neither category is well represented in conventional portfolios. The professionals are usually obliged to follow a careful and well trodden course because their main job is to protect capital rather than take risks with it. The individual small investor can, however, decide precisely what element of risk there should be in his, or her, investments.

My aim in writing this book is, above all, to take an objective view of penny shares and small company investments. The 'pennies' in particular cry out for a calm and reasoned approach – an attitude which many City professionals seem unable to adopt. The simple truth is that in bull markets 'pennies' invariably out-perform the so-called quality stocks and there is no reason why shrewd private investors should not benefit in the process. In a bear market they under-perform, for similarly understandable reasons, so investors must also take that into account. What the private investor should *not* do is succumb to hysteria either way.

1

AN ARMY NINE MILLION STRONG

If you decide to invest in shares you will no longer be joining a small, privileged class. According to research carried out by the International Stock Exchange and the Treasury in 1988, there are almost nine million shareholders in Britain. As government ministers are fond of reminding us, there are now more shareholders than there are members of unions affiliated to the Trades Union Congress. The latest shareholder total represents some 20.5 per cent of the British population over the age of 16.

The number of shareholders has trebled since 1979 (when only 7 per cent of the population held shares). The fall in stock market prices in October 1987 had little effect on this total with most people deciding to hold on to their equities, either out of conviction or because they had little choice. Of the nine million shareholders in 1988, about four million were estimated to hold shares only in privatisation issues, so their commitment to the market cannot be said to be deep. A further half million own shares in the companies which they work for.

The ranks of the serious investors are steadily growing with each year, in parallel with the increase in home ownership (now heading towards the 65 per cent level). The Stock Exchange/ Treasury figures show that 18 per cent of investors have an interest in four companies or more; 27 per cent own shares in two or three companies; while the remaining 55 per cent are invested in just one company. For privatisation issues alone, the figures are 8 per cent with four or more holdings; 28 per cent with two or three; and 64 per cent with just one. Excluding privatisation, an interesting 22 per cent of today's shareholders bought their shares through new issues.

Who are these people? Research shows that 15 per cent came by their holdings through inheritance, gift or other means. Share ownership remains concentrated among the over-40s with many of them representing the 'new rich' who have benefited from the current increase in the value of property. There is also the predictable concentration of ownership in the affluent south-east of England which contains 38 per cent of all the nation's shareholders. The 1988 survey further disclosed that the privatisation programme has spread ownership away from the traditional private investors – the AB socio-economic groups.

The International Stock Exchange (long regarded by the rest of the community as a sort of private club for the privileged) is today in the forefront of promoting wider share ownership. Its then Chairman, Sir Nicholas Goodison, went on record as saying the Stock Exchange wanted to 'remove the mystique of share ownership, to spread the word about how to buy and sell shares, and to help people learn more of the way in which investment works'. The Stock Exchange has even launched an Investors Club for the general public which had 3200 members at the most recent count.

Thus, to the horror of many patrician members, the doors of the Stock Exchange in London and its provincial branches, are theoretically open to all. If you choose to become a member of the Investors Club (annual fee £15) you can vote for the members of your own advisory committee whose voice, it is said, reaches the 'highest level of the Exchange'. There are also seminars, meetings with stockbrokers throughout the country, and a quarterly club magazine. So things have changed a lot in the past year or two.

The Wider Share Ownership Unit is a part of the International Stock Exchange complex in London. It does, however, hasten to point out that it is *not* an investment club. Subscriptions are not invested on behalf of members but are used purely to develop services. The club will not give specific investment advice or stock market tips, so you have to look elsewhere for that. The helpful Wider Share Ownership men and women on the nineteenth floor of the Stock Exchange tower in the City will tell you that you should consider investing in shares but leave the next step to you.

There is plenty of choice with shares in more than 3000 companies being traded daily on the International Stock Exchange. When government stocks, together with traded options, are taken in to account the total number of securities traded exceeds 7000. A recent count showed that 2678 public companies were quoted on the old-established main market; 394 were in the second tier, the Unlisted Securities Market; and 53 fledglings could be found on the Third Market, launched as recently as 1987. In addition there is the informal 'Over-the-Counter' Market operated by dealers outside the Stock Exchange regulations but now being curtailed considerably by the provisions of the Financial Services Act.

How did it all start?

The International Stock Exchange of the United Kingdom and the Republic of Ireland Limited – its formal name today – is an institution with origins in the seventeenth century. The first joint stock, or public company was formed as early as 1553, when money was raised for an expedition to find a north-east passage, upon the recommendation of Sebastian Cabot. Only one ship, captained by Richard Chancellor, reached land in the Bay of Archangel. Russian tribesmen took Chancellor and his crew south to meet the Tsar, Ivan the Terrible, who, anxious to forge closer links with the West, gave Chancellor a trading treaty for English ships.

Chancellor's success with the Tsar led to the formation of the Muscovy Company, the shareholders of which appointed a Governor and Deputy Governor to act for them. That paved the way for the modern joint stock company by separating ownership and day-to-day management. The shares in the Muscovy Company were freely traded and throughout the seventeenth century the practice became increasingly common. In 1694 King William III, seeking funds for the war with France, went to the Bank of England to raise loan stock through public subscription and thereby set the pattern for all future official government borrowing.

By 1697 the first legislation was introduced to restrain the activities of brokers and stockjobbers. These men tended to conduct their business in the City's coffee houses, the best known of them being Jonathan's. Their pattern of business became more formalised in the 1760s when a subscription club was founded at Jonathan's. That friendly meeting place, however, burned down and 'New Jonathan's' opened in Threadneedle Street with members being charged sixpence a day to enter. In 1771 the members voted to change their name to the Stock Exchange.

The first Stock Exchange building was erected on the present site near the Bank of England, the foundation stone being laid in 1801. During the nineteenth century business grew apace, keeping step with the growth of industry and commerce sparked by the

Industrial Revolution. A considerable extension to the building was made in 1884. Parallel with this development, 20 provincial stock exchanges were established and these banded together to form an association in 1890. It was not until 1965 that the process of the federation began which led to the amalgamation of all stock exchanges in the UK and the Republic of Ireland in 1973.

The historic division of brokers and jobbers – which remained for almost 80 years – was formalised in 1908. From that year, members had to be 'brokers' (trading in the market on behalf of clients) or 'jobbers' (wholesalers operating on their own account, but dealing only with brokers). Apart from the first months of the conflict, the market operated throughout the 1914–18 war and enjoyed an unprecedented boom during the 1920s until the Wall Street crash of 1929. The main impact on business, however, came in the early 1930s, the years of world-wide recession and tight credit.

The markets had a slow return to normal after the 1939–45 war and nationalisation of public services and industries dominated the years to 1951. Thereafter, the stock exchanges began to expand in tandem with the post-war growth of the British economy. It was decided in 1961 to replace the old, smaller building with the present 26-storey block – but still on the site first occupied in 1801. The new building was opened by Her Majesty The Queen in 1972 but it was not until the following year that the 23,000 square feet of trading floor came into operation. That year saw, too, the amalgamation of all the country's exchanges into one modern market.

There was an unprecedented fall in share prices in the early 1970s brought about by the inexorable rise in inflation and ceaseless conflict between management and unions in industry. A recovery began in the second half of that decade, however, and by the late 1970s the most sustained bull market in the history of the stock exchange was in full swing. As prices continued to peak, vast sums of money poured into pensions and insurance policies and financial institutions became the dominant investors. By 1980, about 70 per cent of all shares were in the hands of the institutions.

The Stock Exchange today

The present decade has been one of extraordinary expansion and of change. Computerisation replaced the time honoured settlement system and in 1979 the Stock Exchange introduced a radical clearing system known as Talisman. Today, Talisman has a staff of some 750, offices around the world, and handles about 40,000 transactions a day, worth in excess of £1 billion. The watershed year of 1979 also saw the abolition of exchange controls in the UK, enabling British firms to invest on an international basis. But this also exposed British brokers to competition abroad, especially in New York and Tokyo, and it was soon appreciated how under-capitalised most of the London houses were.

During that period the Stock Exchange's historic practices were coming under close government scrutiny in the wake of the Restrictive Trade Practices Act of 1976. The Office of Fair Trading took the view that the Stock Exchange was restrictive in three areas: the operation of a scale of minimum commissions; separation of capacity between broker and jobber; and the old-established restrictions on membership. A major court case, expected to be the longest and most costly in British history, was in prospect. Then, in 1983, an out-of-court settlement was reached whereby the Stock Exchange agreed to abolish its system of minimum commissions by the end of 1986.

That agreement started the chain of events which led to the 'Big Bang' in 27 October 1986 when the market changed its whole mode of operation overnight. Prior to that date restrictions on ownership of member firms were lifted, enabling banks, institutions and overseas companies to acquire stockbroking houses as subsidiaries. Minimum commission scales were abolished, allowing for sharp competition between brokers, and the distinction between brokers and jobbers ended. Since Big Bang, firms have been able to function as 'broker/dealers' (representing clients or buying and selling shares on their own account) and/or 'market makers' (committed to making firm buying and selling prices at all times).

By the time Big Bang arrived, the general public had become aware from television and press coverage, of the appearance of the trading floor in the Stock Exchange. Now the people could see for themselves the conditions under which brokers worked. Since that date, ironically, everything has changed. The trading floor is now a shadow of its former self, occupied by a handful of brokers, dealing face-to-face in the time honoured manner, but mainly used for traded option business.

The 'floor' itself has been replaced by computer screens all over the United Kingdom and Ireland, because of the introduction of a terminal-based quotation system known as SEAQ (Stock Exchange Automated Quotations). Market makers nowadays enter their competing buying and selling prices on SEAQ from their own office terminals. These prices are quickly displayed in the offices of the broker/dealers by means of the Exchange's Topic viewdata network. Trading then takes place, almost invariably, over the telephone. It is a far cry from the friendly, intimate personal contact of the past, but the changes have enabled the International Stock Exchange to stay in the forefront of world trading, with its sophisticated electronic systems handling up to £5 billion worth of business each day.

This then is the vast, increasingly impersonal, organisation with which you will have indirect contact if you decide to enter into the business of buying and selling shares. The International Stock Exchange is concerned with four broad market activities: domestic equities; gilt-edged and company fixed interest securities; options; and foreign equities. You, and millions of small investors like you, are concerned primarily with the first of these.

There are three tiers to the domestic equity market:

1. The old-established market of 'listed' companies, each of which has been obliged in the past to satisfy strict criteria relating to all aspects of their operations.
2. The comparatively new (dating from 1980) Unlisted Securities Market (USM) which is designed to meet the needs of small public companies, such as those considered in this book. The USM is a formal and tightly regulated market.
3. The even more recent Third Market (launched in January 1987) serves still smaller companies, as well as businesses which do not have a wide spread of shareholders. This gives such firms access to equity capital on a regulated basis and should ultimately make it unnecessary for such 'tiddlers' to become involved in dealing with 'over-the-counter' brokers.

Information on all the above markets is carried by Topic, the electronic price information system. A similar system is used for the display of information about government securities (the gilt-edged market) while SEAQ International (available via Topic) exists to carry the input of market makers dealing in foreign securities, thereby strengthening even more London's role on the world financial scene. Each of the four markets is run by a committee of Council members, assisted by experts which supervises all activities in the interests of financial companies and investors, large and small.

An understanding of the Third Market is necessary for anyone proposing to invest in the smallest companies, either directly or via unit trusts or investment trusts. As opposed to the more formal

USM, this market is open to even the youngest of business enterprises. Entry is normally restricted to companies incorporated in the UK but can be extended to enterprises which have not yet commenced trading but can provide information for investors on a well researched product, project or service.

The most typical candidates for the third tier of the International Stock Exchange are companies whose securities have previously been traded off-market by a licensed dealer and which are judged to be of a quality to be offered to the public. The Third Market is open also to newly formed companies with at least one year's trading behind them and a full set of annual accounts. Older firms, too, may qualify if they have recently entered a new business activity and can show at least a year of commercial success in that fresh field.

Companies are normally excluded from admission to the Third Market if the following activities represent more than 10 per cent of their profits or turnover. A holding of cash or near-cash assets; minority stakes in other companies; investment, property or commodity holding or dealing.

A member firm of the International Stock Exchange has to sponsor any application. Such a sponsor takes on big responsibilities in the process, being obliged to guide the company's future conduct in the financial world, and to ensure that ownership is always sufficiently well spread to enable a reasonably liquid market in its shares.

Safeguarding the investor

There are various safeguards for investors. Detailed documents on the firm's ownership and activities have to be filed with the International Stock Exchange and existing shareholders must be advised by circular. Full statistical details must be given to the Exchange Telegraph Company (which provides financial information to a wide circle of clients and the press). Above all, the exchange requires newcomers to provide a 'degree of disclosure which will be sufficient to enable investors to know where a company stands'. Often (in the interests of all concerned) they are obliged to disclose more than the law itself requires to get on to the bottom rung of the International Stock Exchange ladder.

How risky are Third Market companies for the private investor? First of all, it must be pointed out that normally very young enterprises are involved without long track records for investors to judge the quality of management, or the potential of their products or services. In general, therefore, they must be viewed as being more risky investments than those in the Listed or USM tiers of the market. Under the new regime ushered in by the Financial Services Act, broker/dealers are required to demonstrate that any Third Market investment is suitable for the client for whom it is purchased.

Effective self-regulation has always been the proud boast of Britain's stock exchanges. The Financial Services Act puts that traditional activity into a statutory framework, with the aim of combining the speed and flexibility of self-regulation with statutory protection for the investor. It is now a criminal offence to conduct what the law regards as 'investment business' without authorisation. The penalties for carrying on business without such authorisation are severe. Consequently, the investor can part with his money with more confidence although the consequences of the Act are not entirely favourable to the person of modest means dabbling in the market.

Stock market indices

Should you decide to invest, directly or indirectly, in UK or overseas equities you should follow not only the fortunes of your chosen investments but also the ups and downs of the market itself. This requires a broad understanding of the various indices which have been devised to record the overall movement each day and are reported daily in the press and in radio and television bulletins. There are three indices with which you should become broadly familiar:

1. The Financial Times Industrial Ordinary Share Index is the oldest in existence, dating from 1935. It is based upon the shares of just 30 large companies, chosen to be representative of British industry and commerce and is calculated on an hourly basis.

2. The Financial Times Actuaries All-Share Index was introduced in 1962 and covers 746 shares. It is, therefore, that much more sensitive to movements but, because of the size of the spread, it is only calculated on a daily basis.

3. The one you may hear most about is the Financial Times Stock Exchange 100 Share Index which, because of its FT-SE initials, tends to be known by the nickname 'Footsie'. This index dates from January 1984 and is based on the performance of the leading 100 companies listed on the International Stock Exchange. It began with a base value of 1000

and makes use of the most advanced computer technology to give an index which is updated minute by minute, from 9.01 am until about 5.00 pm.

How are the leading 100 companies selected for inclusion in the FT-SE? Broadly speaking, they are the 100 companies with the highest market value, ie the total number of shares issued multiplied by their price. Between them they account for almost 70 per cent of the total value of the market with about three-quarters of them being industrial companies. Changes are kept to a minimum for operational reasons and a company is only dropped if it falls below number 110 in the national ranking. Companies will not be considered if they are resident abroad, are subsidiaries of firms already in the index, have large static shareholdings, or do not pay dividends.

If you do not prove to be a penny share 'wizard', picking shares which appreciate sharply, you may still prosper by being right about movements in the market as a whole. You can exploit such a talent by trading FT-SE contracts on the Traded Options market. Such options are based upon the same concept as applies to individual securities. An index option is designed to enable investors to profit from price movements in the market as a whole, and many investors like the idea. At a recent count, index options accounted for about 10 per cent of the daily contract volume of the traded options market – with FT-SE the most popular area.

2

WHY SHARES ARE INEXPENSIVE

Two front covers of the journal *Investors Chronicle* provide a graphic demonstration of the odd and confusing public image of penny shares. On 20 August 1987 the illustration depicted 'Penny Share Mania' and showed scores of delighted investors piling in to the 'pennies' with obvious excitement and delight. The story inside was couched in euphoric terms,

> 'Bricklayers, judges, housewives – everyone has been punting on penny shares this year. And so far those shares have done stupendously well . . . . However much brokers may glower, so far this year, it's the punters who are laughing all the way to the bank. In the first seven months of 1987 penny shares have done phenomenally well . . . .'

Precisely one year later, in an issue on sale on 20 August 1988, the cover story was 'Penny Share Meltdown' and the artist depicted a giant penny dripping away as though it was made of butter. The comment inside was appropriately gloomy:

> 'Only a year ago penny share punters were having the time of their lives. In a bull market that was itself something of a sensation penny shares were out-performing everything in sight . . . . During the crash penny shares fell further in percentage terms than the overall market . . . . Since then nearly three-quarters of penny shares have continued to under perform'.

It is probably no coincidence that an authoritative financial publication seems to concentrate its attention on penny shares in the month of August, traditionally the 'silly season' in Fleet Street. The high summer period has usually been a time when the tempo of commercial life slows down and real stories are hard to find. Hence the convention that unusual items find their way into the columns of newspapers and journals. Penny shares tend to be ignored all the year round, but why not give them a run in August when there is nothing more interesting to write about? The purpose of this book is to suggest that investment in penny shares, and in smaller companies generally, should be considered seriously all the year round and not seasonally. They are not occasional bonanzas and occasional disasters.

First let me concede that the title of this book could be regarded as being misleading on one level. The securities described *are* 'penny shares' in today's jargon and the companies described *are* 'small', or 'smaller', in the eyes of investment managers in the City of London. But these days there are very few shares which trade at a few pence. My definition of penny shares is therefore those priced at 50p or less. Some people put the limit at 70p, others regard any share still selling at less than 100p as coming within that category.

Similarly people have different ideas about what constitutes a 'smaller' company. Some unit trust managers specialising in this field regard the 'minnows' as those having a market capitalisation of £50 million or less. For others it is £100 million or even £150 million. Those figures may seem on the high side to readers who remember life before the 1970s, but a company can have a capitalisation of £50 million these days and still be operating in a relatively modest way – too small, in fact, even to merit the attention of most stockbrokers. (To arrive at the market capitalisation, simply multiply the number of shares in issue by their price.)

In the USA, the figures are even more striking. There, a 'penny stock' today is usually regarded by professionals as those priced at less than $5 (not far short of £3 at an exchange rate of $1.70 to the pound sterling). Some still describe a 'penny' as being priced at less than $1 but, in fact, shares in that range are normally too high a risk even to be considered. You will have to be prepared to pay several dollars more per share for an investment which has any chance of taking off in the future. There are some 30,000 securities in the 'penny share' (under $5) category across the Atlantic and they are traded on the vast Over the Counter Market (OTC). American 'pennies' occupy a broadly similar position in the USA as in Britain, although the dealing ethics can fairly be regarded as being below those of most UK counterparts.

Creating a penny share

Obviously, it makes sense to acquire a share cheaply and sell it for a higher price. But what makes shares inexpensive? There are, broadly, four main reasons:

1. A public company's share price has slumped following poor results or an obvious blow to the sector in which it trades.
2. A young company's equity is modestly priced because it is in its early days of development and is not employing a treat deal of capital.
3. A new issue of shares is being made, pitched at a level which will attract investors.
4. A large company has decided that its share price has become too 'heavy' and that it should be 'lightened' through a split or a scrip issue.

All the above factors can contribute to the creation of a penny share. Clearly, the new investor is not going to benefit directly from the fourth point above because you already have to be a shareholder to receive a split or a scrip issue. However, the manoeuvre is still worth noting because it explains something of the philosophy behind 'pennies'.

The fact is that most investors like to acquire as large a number of shares as possible for their money. Somehow it is much more satisfying to spend £1000 and get 10,000 shares at 10p each than to spend the same amount of money on 100 shares at £10 each – even though the value of the underlying investment may be identical. It is not just greed which motivates investors. Starting from a tiny base, the 10p share may increase by 10 per cent to 12p as a result of investor interest. It is unlikely that the same sort of rise will occur with the £10 shares, unless something sensational happens to the company concerned.

Companies today are learning to live with 'heavy' share prices, as people slowly become accustomed to the idea of paying more for everything. There is still a strong belief in the City, however, that investors are put off by share prices which are starting to look astronomical. Therefore, finance directors employ one of two ways in dealing with this situation – a share split or a scrip, or capitalisation issue.

A split means that the existing shares in a company are divided without affecting the nominal value of those shares. As an example, take the case of a company whose shares have a nominal, or par, value of £1. They are currently trading at £2.50 in the market

Now the company splits those shares into five, giving each share a nominal value of 20p and new certificates are issued to shareholders. The share price falls from £2.50 to 50p but the investors are no worse off because they now have five times as many shares. The theory here is that the creation of fresh stock or penny shares will bring more buyers into the market and that the split shares will rise in value, perhaps to 60p each. Thus, within a short time, the one share previously worth £2.50 becomes five shares worth £3 collectively.

Such a development is a common feature of high finance and everyone is usually satisfied: the company which is going places in the world; the directors, original shareholders, and new investors who have bought shares in a quoted company whose previous 'heavy' price made them appear unattainable.

A similar situation applies with scrip issues, where a company which has accumulated reserves from past trading profits makes a gift of extra shares to its shareholders. Perhaps one new share is issued for every three already held. Strictly speaking, the shareholders are not being 'given' anything because they already own the reserves. This course of action is simply an accounting device to reward them for their past support. With a scrip, or capitalisation, issue more shares are put into circulation, the price falls initially, but normally recovers to a point above the original level.

Should the penny share investor swoop on such shares after a split or a scrip issue? Although there are bigger potential returns to be made from other 'penny' situations, it often makes sense to seize such an opportunity – but do it quickly, after obtaining what information you can on the company in question. The probability is that you will prosper in time, but the main beneficiaries will, of course, be the shareholders who held the equities before the split or capitalisation. It is, however, all part of the penny share game and you should be prepared to 'dive in' when a solid company reduces the nominal value of its shares. It is normally the action of a confident board of directors and the market reacts accordingly.

The more common reason a public company's share price has slipped into the penny share category is that the market is dissatisfied with its performance. Perhaps it has over extended in purchases and has allocated a large number of shares to satisfy acquisitions which have not performed well. Perhaps profits have slumped or there have been losses for several years. Perhaps most of the assets have been sold and the company has become little more than a 'shell'.

Whatever the reason, an established public company invariably attracts predators, either determined to revitalise the business with their own management and new products or services, or to use it as a vehicle for the injection of new businesses. Here are the areas in which the true penny share investor can operate with profit. A low priced, quoted company inevitably attracts interest and the investor who sees what is happening early enough can go along as the price rises.

Always remember that the Stock Exchange 'quote' itself is very valuable and is the reason why few public companies actually go under completely. A stockbroker friend said recently; 'Every company nowadays has a basic value of £250,000 to £500,000. The minimum cost of going public can be close to £250,000 and it is usually preferable to step into a shell and develop a bombed out business.' For that reason, you can usually invest in a company down on its luck in the knowledge that you are unlikely to lose all your money. It is a gamble, but not to be compared with putting it on a horse.

Lack of City interest

If many shares in these situations rise in price, why are all the City professionals not dabbling in penny shares all the time? The answer is that some of them *are* keen students of 'special situations' and take an active interest in any of their colleagues buying into a loss-making company or a 'shell' company. But most stockbrokers and their clients stay out for the twin reasons that they wish to play it safe and the shares of the companies in question are invariably under-researched.

With financial institutions playing such a major part in the City these days, research is all important. Brokers run large departments of talented and highly paid people whose whole life is spent studying companies and commercial sectors to enable them to make judgements and forecasts. The institutions demand a wealth of information before they acquire shares and brokers tend to restrict their activities to the larger concerns. It is usually not worth carrying out extensive research on smaller companies and besides, the researchers tend to lose interest in those businesses which have run out of steam in recent years.

With costs escalating all the time, the number of companies being analysed (and therefore the subject of major investment decisions) is not growing to an appreciable extent. To survey any public company adequately costs a broker each day between £3000 and £5000 and then that interest has to be maintained in the future. Here is how a highly experienced financial adviser explained it:

> Suppose a broker wants to examine a company in depth. An analyst goes there for a week. His cost will be perhaps £1000 and there will be back-up costs back in the office of around the same amount. There are travel and accommodation expenses and more costs when the analyst returns to the office and makes a report. The bill soon comes close to £5000 in actual cost and overheads.

That is the reason why so many shares are neglected by the major investors and why there is often scope in special situations and smaller companies for the investor with modest means. The broker who has to budget £5000 on a research project is only going to spend that sort of money if it is likely that £500,000 or more will be invested in the company, thus justifying the research and continuous monitoring. Even keeping track of a company already visited by an analyst can be a noticeable ongoing expense.

Information on smaller and up-and-coming companies is not totally denied to private investors. A few stockbrokers do make an effort in this field, but their numbers are declining as their administration costs rise. If you are looking for some kind of research, rather than relying upon your own gleanings and intuition, then you can look to the fund managers of unit and investment trusts operating in the smaller companies sector. They are examining the performances of such companies all the time and are having to work ever harder at it since the post-1987 crash. You obtain the benefit of their research efforts when you acquire their units or shares. The activities of the trusts which are likely to include 'pennies' in their portfolios are studied later in this book.

The Business Expansion Scheme

Turning to another source of inexpensive shares – the new, or very young company – your own local knowledge or contacts may lead you to make an investment in a start-up. Acquiring shares at the outset of an enterprise is sometimes a passport to great prosperity. Many companies start with a capital of just a few thousand pounds, or even a bare £100 and at this stage, a 5 or 10 per cent holding can be very cheap indeed. However, few entrepreneurs are prepared to let others in on the ground floor (unless your acquisition of equity shares is accompanied by a loan) and the mortality rate of new companies is inevitably high. Apart from the rarity of such investments, it is probably best for the small investor to consider the advantages of a Business Expansion Scheme (BES) investment.

Here, you can obtain information on possible holdings by either talking to your accountant (who should be aware of the latest opportunities), subscribing to a specialist publication providing up-to-the-minute information, or by getting on the mailing list of specialist houses who handle BES issues all the time. Some relevant names and addresses are given in Chapter 9. Before considering any participation in this field, do get your own objectives straight. A BES scheme can be a highly profitable investment, but its appeal is to people with above average incomes (and, therefore, looking for the best tax advantage) and it is essentially a long-term transaction.

The BES concept has produced numerous penny share opportunities, some of which have proved very profitable to investors. BES was set up in 1983 with the intention of encouraging enterprise by allowing individuals to invest up to £40,000 in unquoted companies and to offset this against their top rate of tax. Since then well over £700 million has been raised by several thousand companies engaged in almost every conceivable kind of business activity.

Most of the money has gone into asset-backed ventures such as hotels, public houses and shops but a significant amount has been invested in more high risk trading companies. Particularly in the earlier years of the scheme, it was common for such offers to be accompanied by an OTC quotation since this was considered to widen their appeal (even though investors who sell within five years have to pay back the original tax relief). Many of these types of offer also used low price shares to take advantage of the belief that private investors perceive penny shares to offer better 'value'.

The record of these offers has been mixed, perhaps inevitably poor given that most of them were pitched at the riskier end of the market. The 'stars' include Theme Holdings, which graduated to the Third Market and received a takeover bid at a 75 per cent premium to the original price; Specialeyes which has achieved a USM flotation at about three times the original purchase price; and Alan Paul, the Liverpool-based hairdressing chain which is probably currently worth at least five times the amount originally paid by investors.

In the USA a small share price is viewed as being a sign of financial weakness, whereas in the UK it has often been seen as an opportunity for higher capital appreciation. BES investors are forced to take a longer-term view than stock market investors and hence are less attracted by the prospect of a quick return. Therefore, penny share issues have only been a small part of BES activity historically and are likely to remain so in the future.

The following table covers a representative selection of BES penny share issues which spotlights some of the 'hits' and the 'misses':

Company	Sponsor	Price paid (p)	Price at September 1988 (p)
Art Focus	Ravendale	25	0
Applied Engineering Technologies	Security Exchange	15	1
Alan Paul	Capital Ventures	32	150
Audiotext	Tapal	25	12
Country Gardens	—	50	125
Kromographic	UTC	20	16
Investors Newsletters	London & Sussex	15	15
Specialeyes	Baden-Powell Chilcott	27	61
W H Allen	Guidehouse	17	25
P E Kemp	—	27	31
Miss World Clubs	IFICO/Guidehouse	13	6
New Orleans Cafe	Fox Milton	25	0
Panelflex Holdings	Croxley Securities	50	10
Transport Media	Ravendale	20	0
Tomorrows Leisure	Guidehouse	25	29
Telebeam	UTC	40	5
Theme Holdings	Guidehouse	40	70

The above table gives a fair indication of the risks and rewards involved by investing in respectable 'pennies'. Of the 17 securities surveyed, 7 went up in price, 1 stayed where it was, and 9 fell. Remember that these prices reflect the late 1988 situation when the impact of the crash was still having a disproportionate effect on the valuation of smaller companies.

The great privatisation issues have made the general public aware of the fact that they can acquire new shares at source. The nationalised industries have been sold off at generally attractive prices but they have been far from penny share companies. There are, however, new issues from time to time which are not BES ventures and must be considered purely on their merits. Again, you can subscribe to specialist publications in the field or get on the mailing lists of the companies sponsoring the issues. Remember, you must ask for such information and you should not be canvassed.

New share issues

Thousands of small investors put money every year into new issues from companies which are never mentioned in the financial press. Some amateurs do not make any other kind of investment. Often the intention is to 'stag' the issue, ie sell the shares on at a profit as quickly as possible. The ranks of such investors are fairly evenly divided between stock market professionals and the amateurs who rely on making their own judgements on information supplied. One of the tipsheets in the field (*The Penny Share Guide*) also operates a 24-hour telephone tape service, updated daily, which gives basic information on new issues.

Reducing the risks

If you decide to invest in 'pennies', smaller companies and low-priced new issues, then you have to make the basic decision whether to do it yourself or to seek the relative security of having the decision made by a unit or investment trust fund manager. Perhaps the best course of action is a mixture of both, dabbling in 'pennies' on your own initiative (giving instructions to a bank or specialist broker) but also putting part of your faith in the collective investment vehicles. In this way you will be getting a good mix of speculative and relatively safe investments which is the sound principle on which all portfolios should be based.

All investment is a gamble of one kind or another. The great financial institutions, advised by brokers with a wealth of research information behind them, limit the risks as much as possible by investing in companies with proven abilities and enviable track records. But their returns are rarely spectacular, although for most of the time their growth is inexorable. The small investor, however, does not wish to proceed at the same speed. Although the risks are greater, the 'pennies' do offer the prospect of more rapid growth and the opportunity of taking a short cut to a share portfolio of a substantial size.

John Coyne, one of the pioneers of penny share investment, tells of a client of his in the late 1970s, a postman who decided he wanted to become a capitalist. He began by investing £50 a month over a four year period, all of which went into recommended penny shares. Towards the end of the period he extended his out-lay to £100 a month. At the time their association ended (and the postman presumably went on to bigger things) his portfolio was worth £64,000, all made from penny stocks.

Coyne's view is that the essential thing is to take a 'conservative approach to a risky business'. He advocates a spread of penny share investments so that one big loss does not wipe out the port-folio. Then you can look to the good performers and the outstand-ing ones to keep you comfortably ahead of the run-of-the-mill investors. He points out that a share must rise by 20 per cent or more before you make a true profit (taking buying and selling costs into account). Such a percentage rise can be achieved by a 'penny' rising by a small sum of money, say, by around 6p on a share bought at 30p.

The above observation on the need for a sizeable increase in the share price spotlights one of the minus points about penny shares, the dealing spread. When share movements are quoted in the press, or on the television screen, a single price for a share is nor-mally given. This is, in fact, the middle price, a mid-way point between the bid (what you get when you sell shares) and the offer (what you pay to get them) price. This 'spread' is the profit made by the market maker and it is traditionally wide in the case of penny and Third Market shares. Supply and demand determines this fact. The shares of large companies can be traded on narrow margins because they change hands in large quantities and usually because there are several market makers. With the smaller companies, the spread can be sizeable because there is probably just one market maker who can dictate terms.

The spread is one of the reasons why conservative advisers such as bank managers, accountants and solicitors, often warn private investors off investing in 'pennies'. When prices fall the system works more harshly against you than is the case with blue chip shares with narrower dealing spreads. Conversely, it works in your favour when penny shares start to rise and when they do move upwards they often do so at a rate well ahead of big companies with heavier share prices.

The cost of dealing always weighs heavily on small investors, whether or not they invest in 'pennies'. Minimum charges of £20 or £25 are common nowadays and represent fair value but this is a sizeable slice of a £500 investment, especially when you have to pay the same sum when you sell. Some brokers incorporate the

VAT levy in their minimum, others do not. It is always worth checking on this point. There is also the government's charge of a half of 1 per cent stamp duty when you buy. Hence the reason why you do not make a profit until the price of your chosen share has risen by approximately 20 per cent.

There are other reasons for caution. Accounting and reporting standards can be less precise than with the giants of industry, and occasionally a rogue may be at the helm of a small company which appears to be going places. All these points should be taken into account before you decide to invest in penny shares. Go into it knowing that there are hazards, that you can lose part or all of your money, but also that you could do well, enjoy the ride and build the foundations of a modest fortune. Also, as already indicated, if you want to be more cautious, there is smaller company investment available via unit and investment trusts.

Personal Equity Plans

Another thing to consider is that penny shares can yield even higher profits if grouped together in a Personal Equity Plan, or PEP for short. That may sound a surprising suggestion at first reading, for PEPs have tended to be associated with safer and more conventional forms of investment enhanced by the associated tax-free benefits. If you take the decision to concentrate a part of your investment strategy in the penny shares sector then a PEP could still work well for you and add considerably to your profits.

Launched on 1 January 1987 as a way of encouraging more people to invest in British companies, PEPs are available to anyone aged 18 or over and resident in the UK. So long as you keep the money invested in your PEP for the statutory minimum period, it is free of both income and capital gains taxes. (A PEP must be kept for a full calendar year. Thus, if you create a plan in 1989, it must be kept for the whole period between 1 January and 31 December of 1990). It is a simple business. There is no need for you to keep records, or include details of your PEP in your annual return to the Inland Revenue. You can even hold a part of your PEP in cash and earn tax-free interest on that as well.

There is one big proviso. You must have a financial manager, as the government thinking is that new small investors must have the benefit of professional guidance. This is mildly irritating, of course, to experienced investors because it means that management charges are involved. With the prospect of further growth in the economy and rising dividends, the benefits of PEPs (especially if they become an established part of your investment policy) out-weigh the objection to paying fees to an outsider who knows the ropes and has official recognition.

You can contribute to your PEP either monthly or in lump sums. The total amount subscribed in any one January to December period must not be less than £300 nor more than £3000. The smallest lump sum payment is £300, but further £100 amounts can be added at any time up to the maximum limit in the year your plan is opened. There is a minimum of £25 in monthly subscriptions, so the scheme is available to even the smallest investor.

A vast range of management companies offer PEP schemes to the public, including the banks. Most seek to make the investment decisions themselves. They will select the shares, or a mix of shares and unit trusts, and you just sit back and hope the managers will do their work well. Such ready-made schemes are suitable and satisfying for most investors because, after all, an outlay of less than £3000 is not such a big commitment to most of today's investors. Alternatively, provided you appoint a professional manager, you are free to construct a personal PEP to suit your own investment ideas. This certainly makes the whole PEP venture that much more exciting and, possibly, more profitable.

The drawback is that, just as tailor-made suits cost more than ready-made ones, you pay higher management fees if you insist upon making the investment decisions yourself and passing on the orders to the professional. As you might expect, you do not have *carte blanche*. The shares chosen must be listed in one of the International Stock Exchange tiered markets. A total of £540 (or 25 per cent of your subscription, whichever is the higher) can be invested in unit trusts. Joint husband and wife plans are not possible, but each partner can invest £3000 regardless of their personal tax situation.

If you are attracted by the idea of a mix of penny shares and investment in smaller companies, why not construct a PEP in which three-quarters of the money is invested in 'pennies' which take your fancy and the balance in unit trusts invested purely in smaller companies? The returns should be above average, given a continuation of historic trends, and should repay your outlay on higher than usual management charges. So long as you keep within the prescribed limits, you can change your investments as often as you wish. Do not, however, put too many shares into your PEP as dealing costs make the sensible maximum no more than four or five. Income from shares, unit trusts or cash re-invested in your PEP does not affect the £3000 limit.

Any financial intermediary can put you in touch with a PEP management group. All such managers are registered with the Inland Revenue and you can ask them for their regularly updated list of recognised managers. Under the provisions of the Financial Services Act 1986, the managers have to belong to one of the authorised self-regulatory bodies so their financial expertise is assured and, more important, supervised. Chase de Vere Investments (based at 63 Lincolns Inn Fields, London WC2) publish an excellent survey of PEP schemes and will supply this at a modest cost (£2 a copy at time of writing).

A PEP scheme will provide an optimum return if you approach it as a medium to long-term investment, even though you may be making a series of short-term gains within the plan. The value of your tax relief will build up as you start new PEPs in successive years, all within the same tax shelter. There is a good case for arguing that the first £3000 of any investor's risk money should go into a PEP.

3

DO-IT-YOURSELF INVESTMENT

You have doubtless read about Big Bang, and of the advent of the Financial Services Act 1986 which has introduced a new regulatory system covering financial products and services. Perhaps you have read press reports of intensive competition for private business and have concluded that investment as a whole has become simpler and less expensive for the small investor. At the same time, it can be assumed you have concluded that the Financial Services Act has somehow made the whole business of investment safer.

Up to a point, these epochal developments have lived up to the predictions. With the end of the old restrictions on membership of the International Stock Exchange, outside corporations, British and foreign, came on the scene and swallowed up old stockbroking partnerships. The battle for business intensified and lower commission charges became the order of the day. Since the October 1987 downturn in international markets the in-fighting has become even more intense. Margins are becoming wafer thin, and the City expects some of the weaker companies to cease trading.

But has the small investor really benefited from Big Bang? The answer must be 'not directly'. The main beneficiaries of the lower commission charges have been the major institutions for whom dealing has become considerably cheaper. At the same time, in a relatively short period, private business has become expensive and unattractive for stockbrokers. Firms are closing down their private client divisions, or putting them up for sale. All are seeking clients with larger and larger sums to invest.

The traditional sources of advice and help for the private investor are, therefore, shrinking dramatically. Happily, however, other doors are opening continually. Once upon a time, the small investor had to rely upon the historic prices in the daily newspapers for information. Today, a plethora of instant information is available at modest cost. The near monopoly of stockbrokers has been broached by banks and building societies, telephone dealing operations and share shops. Everything is quicker, more open, and should be cheaper – but many investors are finding that they cannot get much professional help.

The Financial Services Act

This big switch to a do-it-yourself situation was surely not envisaged by the serious and well-meaning people who drafted the Financial Services Act. They were concerned simply with creating a new regulatory framework to protect investors, in an era in which the financial services industry was growing rapidly and diversifying widely. There is no doubt that the old legislation, the Prevention of Fraud (Investments) Act of 1958, was in need of reform.

Before noting how and why many private investors are being, and will be, thrown on to their own resources, it is necessary to look briefly at the provisions of the Act. It is now law that anyone carrying on investment business in the UK must be authorised as a 'fit and proper' person to do so. It is a criminal offence to carry on business covered by the Act without such authorisation. Breach of this law can result in imprisonment for two years.

The Act delegates powers to the Securities and Investments Board (SIB), and various organisations which it in turn recognises, to ensure that investment businesses are honest, solvent and competent and remain so. Investments covered by the legislation include stocks and shares, unit trusts, life insurance policies where there is a return on the premium (such as endowment schemes linked to mortgages), personal pensions, gilts, futures, commodities, debentures, warrants and options. Excluded are bank and building society deposits (regulated by separate legislation) and investments in such items as property, wine, precious metals and stones, stamps, commemorative coins, mugs, plates and so on.

The self-regulatory body whose work is of most relevance to the private investor is FIMBRA (The Financial Intermediaries, Managers and Brokers Regulatory Association). Its job is to regulate those firms which offer independent investment services to the general public. At the time of writing, it appears that FIMBRA will ultimately have rather more than 9000 members. These member firms either deal with the public as agents (arranging investments with a third party) or as principals (buying investments in their own names and selling them on to clients).

Companies are scrutinised closely before being admitted to membership of FIMBRA. Once it becomes a member, a firm of investment advisers must report its financial position at least once a year and have its accounts checked by an independent auditor. FIMBRA reinforces this operation by carrying out random checks on members, with firms handling clients' money being visited more often than less complex businesses. Such visits are not only designed to check that accounting rules are being observed; the manner in which the business is being conducted is also surveyed.

There are detailed rules to be observed, too, on advertising, the literature given to the public, and on recording the advice which is given to clients. All in all, FIMBRA operates with the laudable aim of ensuring, as far as possible, that clients are offered suitable, independent and competent advice, and that investment firms do not run into financial difficulties, hazarding clients' money in the process.

This elaborate regulatory framework, of which FIMBRA is part, cannot remove all risk from investment. There is a potential risk in every type of investment. Prices can go down as well as up, dividends may be lower than expected, or passed, and enterprises issuing shares can collapse. There is no way of protecting the investor from every risk and FIMBRA members are supposed to suggest to people unwilling to accept any kind of setback, that their capital would best be placed with institutions offering interest on deposits, such as banks and building societies.

FIMBRA, above all, places upon its members the responsibility of giving clients 'best advice' and, with the best will in the world, this is very difficult to achieve. Among the co-operative forms of investment alone, there are more than 1200 unit trusts and some 160 investment trusts to take into account. Throw in all the insurance company products, National Savings and government securities, and the total of possible forms of investment becomes mindboggling. Few stockbrokers will advise on any security in the penny share category. So how does 'investment off the beaten track' fit into the brave new world of regulation?

The short answer is that the penny share investor must remain outside the fold, obtaining his or her own information and making personal buying and selling decisions. The same situation, broadly, applies to investing in the shares of smaller companies on the three tiers of the International Stock Exchange. There can be some protection for the investor interested in reaching smaller companies via unit trusts or investment trusts. Here, the services of a professional adviser and FIMBRA member might be retained but in such cases the usual reaction is likely to be a suggestion that it becomes 'execution only business', where the intermediary is not accepting responsibility for giving the relevant advice.

So there is the reason for the heading to this chapter. Investment in penny shares is very much a do-it-yourself business, largely unaffected by all the massive changes that have taken place in consumer protection. To all intents and purposes you are still on your own! When you invest it will be 'execution only' most of the time without the protection that is accorded to more conventional investors under the Financial Services Act. You have been warned. It is thus essential that you first make up your mind about the desirability of considering the investments mentioned in these pages, and then ascertain just how you can 'do it yourself'.

Sources of information

Happily, doing it yourself is a far more exciting, and less onerous, business these days than it once was. If you seek to use an intermediary, the field is better regulated than ever. On the other hand, services now proliferate through which you can receive the necessary information speedily and in the comfort of your home. Today, you deal in a bitterly competitive market where the practitioners are obliged to offer commission rates which would formerly have been regarded as inadequate. The number of outlets where trading can take place has increased to an almost bewildering extent. At the same time, however, you can play the market from your armchair seven days a week.

The Securities and Investments Board

First, let us assume you are seeking the services of a stockbroker. As we have observed, the International Stock Exchange these days is very helpful and will supply literature and lists of brokers who will accept private clients. In practice, however, few will be interested in dealing in penny shares and you will find the select list in Chapter 9 useful in this regard. Should you seek the services of a professional adviser, then the first do-it-yourself step is to consult the Central Register of the Securities and Investments Board.

This can be done from your own home by means of Prestel, the electronic information service. If you have a computer (or TV set with adaptor) you already have access to Prestel. If not, many public libraries have machines for public use. Access to the register on Prestel costs 30p per name checked, but there may be a further charge for use of a library machine. Alternatively, you can write to the SIB at their London headquarters (address given in Chapter 9).

Authorised firms under the new rules are regulated by a number of bodies: the SIB itself, various self-regulating organisations (SROs) and recognised professional bodies (RPBs). Details of each of these bodies can be found in the Central Register so you can always be sure you are dealing with a properly authorised company, or individual. The Register entry gives full details of all firms covered by the regulations, their authorisation status, its regulatory body, and a brief description of the main type of investment business which it conducts.

The names of individual salesmen, representatives or agents of authorised firms do not appear on the Register. This is because their employer has to take full responsibility for investment business activity. Any such person, however, must disclose to you the name of his or her employer. If you are worried about potential rogues, then you may find their names among the list of prohibited persons – those officially disqualified from working in the financial services industry. The Register also contains details of all authorised unit trusts and overseas recognised collective investment schemes which can be marketed legally to the British public.

Today there is an embarrassment of riches for the small investor seeking information. Some sources only require the use of your own telephone, perhaps adapted at modest cost, to obtain round-the-clock price information and market reports. Other call for more elaborate and expensive equipment, but still within the means of most people taking a serious interest in the investment game. All the most advanced technology of the late 1980s can be acquired for your personal use from the numerous specialist companies now providing sophisticated information.

Some small investors may feel more at home dealing with established and well known institutions such as building societies and national newspapers. There is good news for such people. Both are closely involved in the post-Big Bang world, with some building societies ready to trade in shares for you, and the newspapers to provide you with round-the-clock information. (Their addresses are also given in Chapter 9.)

Building societies

Building societies have been able to widen their activities considerably as a result of the sweeping provisions of the 1986 Building Societies Act. That legislation gave societies powers to acquire land, build houses, buy or start up estate agencies, offer chequebook and related services and launch such products as unit trusts, PEPs, and pension schemes. The idea was to make them better placed to face the competition from other financial institutions which had been eroding their traditional home lending market.

A few societies have linked with established stockbroking firms to deal in shares for clients. The National & Provincial Building Society, for example, has teamed up with Allied Provincial Securities, one of the largest regional stockbroking firms in the UK. Customers are asked to complete a form and are then given a share-dealing card. With that card they can either buy or sell stocks and shares at branches of the Society, or trade over the telephone to a limit of £5000 per transaction. There is a £5 joining fee and thereafter the customer pays the standard commission claimed by the stockbrokers.

Many branches of the Bristol & West Building Society offer share dealing services under an arrangement with Laing & Cruickshank, whose staff actually work in the Society's Bristol and Worcester premises. Free telephone links make their advice available to customers in other Bristol & West branches. New investors, as well as established customers, can use the facilities and those with money invested in the Society continue to earn interest right up to settlement day.

Investors with the Cheltenham & Gloucester Building Society can deal in the largest and most commonly traded equities through a link with Barclays De Zoete Wedd Securities. You need to have, or to open, one of the Society's 'Gold Accounts' and all transactions are recorded on that account. One of the claims made for this service is that the commission is modest – £18 minimum on transactions up to £2000; 1 per cent for deals between £2001 and £10,000 and a flat £100 thereafter. But it is strictly 'execution only' and only Alpha or Beta stocks (see Chapter 8) are covered – so it is not the place for a penny share investor.

On the other hand, all securities traded on the International Stock Exchange and the USM can be bought and sold at branches of the Norwich and Peterborough Building Society. The service is operated in conjunction with two East Anglian stockbrokers but is a trading only service – no advice is given. You have to be an investing member of the Society to participate. Minimum commission quoted is £25 on both shares and gifts.

In Scotland, the Dunfermline Building Society offers a similar scheme, operated in tandem with stockbrokers Bell Lawrie. Applications for new issues are said to be especially welcome in that Society's branch offices. Purchases and sales are recorded in your account with the society but, once again, it is an 'execution only' arrangement. You make the decisions. As might be expected north of the border, a competitive commission is quoted – 1.65 per cent with a minimum of £20.

Newspapers

Newspapers have been the traditional sources of share price information for private investors. These days they also compete to provide you with up-to-the-minute prices and information around the clock. Six newspapers – the *Financial Times*, *The Times*, the *Daily Telegraph*, the *Guardian*, the *Independent*, and the *Observer* – are in the market to serve you. Their respective telephone numbers are given in Chapter 9. These are excellent and efficient services, but they are not free and you must appreciate that using them will push up your quarterly telephone account.

At this point, it should be observed that one of the new investor's first duties these days is to learn something about the very commercial telephone system operated by British Telecom. The first figures of a number are a clue to what it will cost. A number which begins with 0800 is completely free. One that begins with 0898 or 0077 is a premium rate service and that is billed at 38p per minute (peak) and 25p per minute (off peak); so take account of such rates when seeking information on the stock market. Obtaining a market report can cost you about half as much as calling the US.

Nevertheless, the various newspaper services are very useful for the armchair investor. The first in the field was the *Financial Times* which now operates as FT Cityline. By telephoning the service you can obtain up-to-the-minute prices on 3500 shares, current prices on 6000 unit trusts, insurance funds and other investments, and a choice between 29 market reports, at home and abroad. You work with share and unit trust directories (provided free). There is also FT Cityline Portfolio Plus, under which you receive a personal account number enabling you to register your investments with the FT computer. Then, at any time, you can dial up the present price of each share or unit trust and ascertain the total value of your portfolio. It costs £5 to register and there is a £5 annual subscription.

The *Independent* Index, the most recent in the field, is essentially the same as the *Financial Times* service, but with the embellishment of an investment game for readers (if the idea of playing with notional sums of money appeals to you). To use the FT Cityline, you need to have a modern touch-tone telephone, or a pocket-size tone generator which is placed across the mouthpiece of an ordinary telephone. The same equipment is required for the *Daily Telegraph* Teleshare Service which similarly connects you into the heart of the Stock Exchange Automatic Quotations System (SEAQ).

The Teleshare facility converts the electronic signals from SEAQ into human speech, providing you with price information precisely as it is becoming available to the professionals. The *Daily Telegraph* system, too, enables you to specify the information you require by using the keys on your telephone, or the tone generator. A £10 subscription to the *Daily Telegraph* runs for a year and includes a membership card and binder, an index of shares, and a tone generator. Prices of around 4000 shares and securities are covered.

Guardian Sharecall also receives its information from a company known as Telephone Information Services, providers of the basic 'Teleshare' service. It offers similar facilities to readers and was preparing to add unit trusts to the register as this book went to press. *Observer* Business Line is similarly linked to the SEAQ fed from the International Stock Exchange and is accessed by telephone. Investors with an MF telephone or a tone generator are provided with real-time share prices and a portfolio service.

The national newspapers do not initiate all this information themselves but obtain it from specialist companies such as Telephone Information Services or the British Telecom Citycall operation. *The Times* Stockwatch is provided in conjunction with BT Citycall and gives the latest trading prices of some 10,000 stocks, shares, gilts, unit trusts, offshore funds and bonds, insurance and pension funds. As with other services, you need a multi-frequency telephone or a tone generator. If you elect to register your personal portfolio with Stockwatch, then you can access it any time by keying in a number and secret password. (Up to 25 items can be stored on each password.)

Electronic sources
The national newspapers, of course, have latched on to large, established services and you can instead go straight to the various sources of information. British Telecom's Citycall, launched in February 1985, has been a pioneer in the field and was, in fact, the

first of all the premium telephone services. It has been available on a nation-wide basis since April 1986.

Citycall's primary service, Financial Bulletins, produces about 400 bulletins every day. These services can be accessed from anywhere in the UK by telephoning a pre-set number. The market commentaries are usually updated every half hour but some use the latest voice processing technology. These take share prices direct from a real-time live database every few minutes and create audio reports. Although the voices sound real they are actually generated by computer.

In addition to the bulletins, Citycall offers a real-time share information facility called Citycall Portfolio (as mentioned in the previous note on *The Times*). Some 11,000 prices are available covering quoted and USM shares, unit trusts and other managed funds. As with the newspaper services, there is no charge – British Telecom makes its money from the use of the telephone system. A recent improvement in the service has been the facility for advising investors whether unit trusts are priced 'forward' or on an historic basis.

The rival Teleshare service offers information on around 4000 shares. As with the British Telecom facility, it is available seven days a week, 24 hours a day. Your basic membership is free but, for £10 a year, you get a full index and user guide together with the necessary pocket-sized tone generator to function in tandem with your own telephone.

If you have access to British Telecom's Prestel network then you should consider Citiservice, managed by a firm called ICV Information Systems. Using an ordinary telephone line you can dial into this service using an adapted television set, a dedicated terminal, or a personal computer in your home. You can call up on screen the current prices of around 10,000 gilts, equities, unit trusts, insurance funds and other securities. As a private investor you pay £42 a quarter for the use of this facility.

Prestel also offers the possibility of electronic dealing and telebroking. If you are a member, and have a broker who participates in the scheme, you can access his commentary, research and recommendations at any time. Having made your investment decision, to buy or to sell, you place your order via the system. As soon as the market opens your broker will deal with your order and send you a 'Prestel Mailbox' message confirming the transaction. So if you lead a very busy life with little time to talk to your broker, you can still dabble in shares or unit trusts while sitting in front of the family television. As with other services, you can register your own portfolio on Citiservice and have it revalued every evening.

Banks and other financial advisers
Services such as Prestel, however, are for the dedicated investor rather than the great majority who have still committed little to the market. (A broker recently said that three-quarters of those now recognised as shareholders have staked £600 or less to date.) For the smaller fry, the professionals acknowledge that (for all their own interest in obtaining commission earnings) the best recommendation may finally be to use your own high street bank. All the major banks are now heavily into share-dealing and their charges are generally competitive.

The drawbacks are that they will not be able, or willing, to give advice on penny shares and out-of-the-ordinary investments and they may not always be quick off the mark in getting your order into the system. But their charges can be reasonable. Lloyds and the Midland have minimum commission charges of £20 while National Westminster quotes £25, except for sales below £125 where the charge is 20 per cent of the investment. Thus, for the small investor, the bank can be the answer and at some NatWest branches there are screens where you can view the latest prices of a restricted number of equities. Times are indeed a-changing!

While most stockbrokers will not welcome you with open arms if you express a keen interest in dabbling in penny shares, some will and one firm prepared to listen with sympathy is Stock Beech & Company, with offices in Bristol, London and Birmingham. They say they are 'prepared to invest less than others'. Their own costs tend to be lower than the big London brokers because of their provincial base with their minimum charge at £25 plus VAT per transaction. Normally they are looking to handle an investment of £1000 but will come down as low as £500. Such business is, of course, on an 'execution only' basis and no advice is given.

When considering minimum commissions in the £20 to £25 range, it must be remembered that office costs have soared considerably in recent years and especially since Big Bang, when there was a scramble to find good people at almost any salaries. Some of the top London stockbrokers now reckon that each transaction costs them £70 to £80 in administration and back-up costs. Hence the tendency for some of the patrician houses to get rid of their private business, as gently as possible.

Stockbrokers operate in our larger cities and investors living in the country may well consider the newish Fidelity Share Service which promotes itself as being 'cost-efficient' broking for the experienced investor. It is an 'execution only' operation which is aimed at people who already have some knowledge of the market. There is a joining fee of £25, after which the commission rate is £25 on deals below £1400, rising to £50 in the £4000 to £20,000 bracket and negotiable thereafter.

Fidelity will provide you with facts and prices but will not give advice. It undertakes to contact any market maker on your behalf, so this could be useful for the penny shares investor. The company is happy to deal in USM, Third Market and OTC stocks. As a nominee-based service, Fidelity does all the paper work for you and this should ensure prompt buying and speedy settlement when you sell. It is one of the giants in the field and generated more commission income in 1987 than any other company in the City. Here is a case of a large firm which can be good for the small investor. However, do not register with Fidelity if you are planning to make only occasional deals as there is an administration charge if you become inactive.

You may lack the confidence to enter into 'execution only' business at the outset and, especially if you are thinking of going into unit trusts or investment trusts, it may make sense to approach a professional adviser. The desirability of receiving independent financial advice is at the heart of the Financial Services Act. Advisers who are free of links with product companies have banded together in an organisation called the Campaign for Independent Financial Advice (CAMIFA). It is backed by 14 leading life insurance companies which collectively account for more than 40 per cent of the UK's life and pension industry.

If you feel strongly about the need for independent advice then you can identify a CAMIFA practitioner by a distinctive logo displayed at the place of business. In itself this symbol does not guarantee protection for the consumer (or advice which will necessarily be profitable) but it does confirm that the intermediary is not a representative of a single life office or a unit trust firm.

In practice, however, the average CAMIFA professional will not be able to help much with investment in low-priced shares, although he or she should be able to give you objective information on unit trusts and investment trusts which are invested in smaller companies.

4
SOME TIPS ON THE TIPSTERS

The ranks of penny share investors have declined appreciably during 1988. Their numbers have probably halved since 19 October 1987 – 'Black Monday' – now in City lore. And those still there have been investing far less than they were in the heady days of 1987. Penny share enthusiasts say it has been a 'mediocre year' for their favourite type of investments; critics comment that the 'pennies' have 'performed abysmally'.

So why suggest that anyone should remove hard-won cash from a building society to acquire a stake in such a lacklustre market? To give an adequate answer to that sensible question we must go back to the start of the recent problems – the violent price movements which are commonly described as the 'stock market crash' or 'the collapse of world markets'. So let us now look at what the tipsters say.

As this book was being written, the M & G Group, Britain's leading unit trust managers, were putting to brokers the argument that the events from Black Monday onwards were 'no more than a correction, albeit an unusually large and rapid one'. M & G were driving home this point by illustrating their message with the chart which appears on page 49. As you will note, the overwhelming lesson to be learned from it is that share prices *do go up* (bull market), despite the dips (usually of short duration) which the City calls a bear market. In the quarter century or so since 1962 the general movement has been strongly upwards.

The M & G commentary is so apposite and sensible that it is worth quoting a few paragraphs from it:

The events of last October have inevitably left their mark on investor confidence. They say your first big bull market is like your first love affair – you never forget it – and there is still an air of mourning among many inhabitants of the financial area for the loss of the heady days of last summer. However, it is perhaps true to say that insofar as there has been a bear market over the past few months, it has been in the financial service business, not the stock market, and recent poor sentiment has probably had as much to do with City redundancies and bonus cuts as with economic fundamentals.

Without denying the uncertainties of the future, let us try to restore some perspective. . . . The big trend is in our favour despite periodic bad times of deflation and slowing growth. Nor is this particularly surprising since equities are a slice of the real economy and this tends to grow over the years, cycles notwithstanding.

. . . we have always maintained that October's falls were no more than a correction, albeit an unusually large and rapid one.

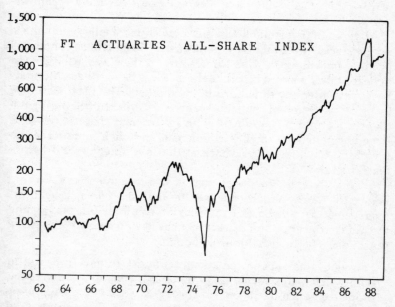

Share prices keep on rising, despite the occasional dip. This graph, produced by the M & G Group, traces the rise in the FT Actuaries All-Share Index between 1962 and 1988. In particular, it puts in perspective the crash of 1987 which caused so much shock and despondency at the time.

... Painful as the correction proved to be, in many respects it could be regarded as a good thing, shattering the widespread illusion that equity investment over a short period is a one-way bet. This illusion was fostered by the exceptional strengths of all markets in the mid-eighties and was further nurtured in the UK by the privatisation issues which not only suggested the possibility of risk-free capital gains, but also helped obscure the basic concept of a share as an entitlement to a future stream of income. This is particularly ironic since, as we have just mentioned, long-term investment in equities is probably the nearest you are likely to get to a one-way bet. ...

Sadly those passages were addressed only to brokers, not to the public at large. Small investors are rarely addressed in such simple and practical terms in the lay press. They do need to be told the basic facts of commercial life because only then can the individual without City connections or experience make a realistic investment decision. The day of investment in equities being a long term, one-way bet is returning. Perhaps by the time you read these words this fact will have become more widely acknowledged.

All types of investment, whether blue chips, smaller companies, penny stocks, unit and investment trusts, will benefit as conditions become bullish again. Good times are on their way back for the investor but it will not be precisely as it was before Black Monday. It never is after any downturn in the markets. The inexorable rise in prices is resumed, but the scenario is different. Some of the theories behind this are dealt with in the next chapter, which is largely devoted to smaller companies and their importance to investors. But first, a look back at the investment world before Black Monday.

1987 was certainly a spectacular year for penny stocks. Writing before the stock market collapse, the *Investors Chronicle* acknowledged that penny shares had 'run riot, routinely out-performing the indices during a bull market that has itself been something of a sensation'. The financial journal added:

You would have been remarkably unlucky to have invested in penny shares this year and lost money. The gamblers' den of the Stock Exchange has been, for this brief period, safe as houses. ... You could have made a fortune. Most people didn't, of course, but quite a few made a respectable amount of money, some by doing their homework and picking their pennies conscientiously, others by sticking a pin into a list of companies whose share prices were 'cheap'. There is still money to be made by the former approach but the latter we would discourage.

The journal looked again at the same companies a year later. By then, two had gone into liquidation leaving 48 to be surveyed. Of those, 38 under-performed the FT All Share Index between the days immediately before the crash and late August of 1988. It commented, 'To say that penny shares outperform 'quality' stocks in bull markets and under-perform them in bear markets is to repeat what seasoned investors already know (or should), that penny shares are more volatile than other shares. When they move at all, they move fast. That, and the low price, are the penny share's greatest attractions.'

Further confirmation of how well the penny stocks did in the last bull market comes from this study of the top performing shares (drawn from every quoted company on the UK stock market) for the period 1 January 1987 to 12 November 1987, when the market was around its lowest point for the year. Of the 10 leaders, eight were penny shares by my definition of 'less than 50p':

Company	Price 1.1.87	Price 12.11.87	% change
	(p)	(p)	
George Ingham	6.5	110	+ 1592
Seafield	5.0	60	+ 1100
Acsis Jewellery	9.35	90	+ 863
Mersey Docks Comb	31.0	268	+ 765
Ecobric Holdings	10.0	73	+ 630
Entertainment Production Services	3.98	25	+ 529
Oakwood Group	88.0	525	+ 497
Excalibur Jewellery	13.32	68	+ 411
Pavillion Leisure	63.0	313	+ 397
Pacific Sales	45.0	215	+ 378

Of course, the above stocks have fallen back since, in the general decline in which the pennies have suffered most. The profits were made by those who took them during a period in which money was pouring in to all kinds of equities at a fantastic rate. Such profits were taken, both by private investors and by canny institutions which sold large holdings on to the small fry at peak prices. Many penny stocks were left with the market makers and this has been a considerable drag on the market during 1988.

Tip sheets

Some penny share investors have, however, continued to make profits since the crash. Both the leading tip sheets in the field are able to boast useful successes during 1988. *Penny Share Guide*'s editor, John Snowden, listed a string of tips in the difficult market which should have made money for his subscribers. He made these claims while conceding that it had been a 'fairly mediocre period' for them all.

When asked for chapter and verse, he gave a number of documented examples. *The Penny Share Guide* had tipped Ellis & Goldstein at 60p and it went to 130p between March and July of 1988. William Jacks, one of 25 shares tipped as most likely to double in price during the year, was recommended at 56p and went to 96p between January and August. The tipsheet recommended Infrared Associates at 36p in July and was giving 'sell' advice at 70p inside a month or so. Investors who followed the advice to buy Optometrics at 15p in May could have sold at 35p in August. Other 'pennies' had gone up by modest percentage points but editor Snowden admitted recovery generally was still slow.

John Gommes, editor of *Penny Share Focus*, told a similar story of some investors being able to get good value in the depressed market of 1988. He confirmed that 'quite a few' of their recommendations had doubled in price since Black Monday, but conceded there had been 'nothing like Polly Peck'. There will still be opportunities about in 1988 and there would be more in 1989 – 'penny share opportunities always exist'. But Gommes asserted that it all had 'nothing to do with the stock market' which was all about obtaining good apparent value. With 'pennies', the main interest was in small companies where 'something was going to happen'. Perhaps a fresh management was coming in, new products were being introduced, or a shell was being revitalised. He defined the basic philosophy behind penny shares as follows.

First, there is the upside potential from a small base, especially where a shell operation is involved. Second, there is a limited downside because of the high value of a stock market quote and the relative ease of analysing a balance sheet versus the profit and loss account.

Both tipsheets, perhaps inevitably, see the present as a good time to invest in 'pennies', especially those prepared to wait patiently for a time to obtain good value for their investments.

How are these investors operating? *Penny Share Guide* research indicated that more than half their subscribers used brokers. Many placed their orders through banks. However, the big problem in dealing via banks remains that they passed the business on to others and there were often delays while customers' orders were assembled for despatch to brokers. Consequently, time was often lost in carrying out buying or selling orders. There was also the problem that messages went down the line so that, if the broker had a query or required fresh instructions, it all had to come up the line again to the customer.

Anyone subscribing to a penny share tip sheet will become accustomed to broadsides being fired regularly at brokers and at the national newspapers, which often patronise or criticise the tipping fraternity. The case against brokers is that they research only the leading companies, mainly for institutional clients, and ignore the vast majority. The tip sheets claim they are filling that research gap to the best of their ability.

A recent example of this was an up and coming British industrial company which had as its broker one of the best known names in the City. This company, capitalised at less than £10 million, had some £2 million in the bank with profits likely to quadruple to more than £1 million in the current year. But the share price was low and few investors seemed to know of its existence or potential. When *Penny Share Guide* wrote about them, the firm invited the tip sheet to make a full survey of their activities because 'we cannot arouse any interest in our own brokers'. For the patrician stockbroking firm the company retained, it was too small and not a commercial proposition.

The treatment of private clients in the matter of fees is another issue frequently ventilated in the tip sheets. With market makers relying on financial institutions for almost 80 per cent of their business, all the cuts in commission rates are benefiting the 'big boys'. Some of them pay just 0.2 or 0.3 per cent for their volume transactions, whereas a typical commission charged to the private investor (if he is being kept on the books at all) is around 1.65 per cent and rising.

Changing the image

Previously, neither the friends nor the critics of the tip sheets have credited them with being particularly strong on the research side. A general feeling has been that the compilers of the sheets rely chiefly on the odd inspired leak, intelligent guesswork, or chance their arms on the slimmest of information. In fact, one of the consequences of the Financial Services Act has been to oblige the tip sheets to carry out detailed research on any company they recommend. Both *Penny Share Guide* and *Penny Share Focus*, as providers of investment advice, have obtained membership of FIMBRA and are bound by the regulations of that body.

Having smarted for years under sniping from Fleet Street newspapers, the tip sheets nowadays assert that the quality of their advice outstrips that of even the 'quality' press. As *Penny Share Guide* told readers in an editorial, 'If we have a hunch about a company, we now have to say it is a hunch and therefore a speculation. Unlike journalists in the national press who can tip a company without having written back-up to prove they have researched the fundamentals'. On pages 55–6 you will find a form used by the *Penny Share Guide*. This has to be completed by any contributor making a recommendation to readers. As can be seen, it is a detailed document requiring a great deal of work before a tip can be made in print. No story is printed until such a form has been checked by the editor. No contributor is paid for an article until he or she has completed the form properly. Whether the information printed proves ultimately to be a profitable comment or otherwise for subscribers, they can be assured that skill and effort have gone into it.

There is official force behind this procedure. All such forms are kept on file and may be checked by a FIMBRA inspector. Such visits can be made at any time and it is thought that inspections of tip sheet records will take place several times a year. This must be regarded as something of a landmark in the annals of British journalism. One shudders to think what would be the reaction of most national newspaper staff if they were compelled to log so carefully all the contacts they had made and all the sources consulted before writing any 'think piece'. The new strictures on the tipsheets must in time add to their stature and in the way they are viewed by the whole financial services community.

A firmly held view of the tip sheets is that they are strong on advice to dabble in penny shares, but short on cautionary notes and warnings. Again, this is less true than it was, partly because of their FIMBRA membership. They are also able to point to some of their pre-crash editions and to comment 'do not say we did not warn you'. *Penny Share Guide* issued warnings to readers about the over-heated market in July and August of 1987. The August comment was explicit, 'When penny stocks suddenly jump to pounds just because some guy has bought a 5 per cent or a 25 per cent stake, the system is over-heating which will one day lead to burnt fingers, especially among the more amateur investors who have never known a bear market. Remember a profit is not a profit until it is in the bank.'

FSL/NISG/USM/OTC/ VENTURE OPINION/PSG/AM CHART/ USM INV/OTHERS

COMPANY NAME: . . . .

Co Address . . . .

. . . .

FULL/USM/OTC/BES/US/OTHER . . . .

Price (as at   .   .   ) . . . .

Prices Quoted   FT . . . . D Tel . . . .

Shares Issued: . . . . Dir's hldgs % . . .   Other lge hldgs % . . . .

Mkt Cap at latest price . . . .

Share Price: High . . . . .Low . . . .

Basic Activities . . . .

. . . .

Results: Finals . . . . Interims . . . . AGM . . . .

Year-end Date:	Current/ Historic Year	Current/ Prospective Year
. . . . Turnover	. . . .	. . . .
Pretax Pft	. . . .	. . . .
EPS	. . . .	. . . .

Latest Interims	Previous	Latest	ESTIMATED NET
Date . . . . .Turnover	. . . .	. . . .	ASSET VALUE
Pretax Pft	. . . .	. . . .	PER SHARE
Tax	. . . .	. . . .	. . . .
EPS	. . . .	. . . .	

Precis of Chairman's Statement: ....

....

....

....

....

....

Other Company Indications/orders etc

....

....

....

....

....

Comparative Co

historic price/earnings

....

....

....

....

....

....

....

....

....

Article prepared after:

Contact with Company   Y/N Who .... Tel No ....

With Company's Broker Y/N Who .... Tel No ....

Company Visit   Y/N When ....

Own Research   Y/N

Signed .... Date ....

In September it commented, ' . . . you simply must keep your head about you even though all else may be losing theirs. Remember no one is that clever. At this rate it can't go on. Keep taking some profits and keep setting the stop-losses and then keeping to them.'

These comments have been quoted to show that the tip sheets can be far more responsible than many people consider them to be. But what are the pitfalls of basing at least some of your decisions on a weekly publication, especially one that may have lost part of its topicality during the production period? This is a constant bugbear with the sheets. Critics assert that by tipping shares they often create artificial markets and that numerous people 'pile in' automatically as soon as the shares can be bought or sold on a

Monday morning. Also, at least among brokers, there is a common criticism that tip sheet employees are often interested in the shares they recommend.

It is quite true that artificial markets can be created by such tips, although the same can apply to newspaper comments, broker circulars and off-the-cuff statements by company chairmen. So far as the investing by staff is concerned, a tip sheet is required to disclose this whenever a share is recommended. This is done in the body of the report or a statutory note on the back page of the publication. It is not a cause for suspicion. Remember that directors of the companies named may themselves be investing, quite properly, and they will know more than the tipster (and probably have far more to invest).

The point to remember always is that the shrewd investor buys and sells on market prices which do not necessarily reflect fully the cold reality of a situation. The fact that thousands of people read the same tip during a weekend is not necessarily an inhibiting factor. What regularly happens is that the share price in question does respond quickly to a tipsheet recommendation. But, as often as not, the price later steadies. At that point, it is often the best time to buy, just before a steady move forwards. This second burst has been a common scenario with 'pennies'. There is no need to be unduly depressed because so many people share the same information on a Saturday and Sunday.

No one would suggest that the penny share tip sheets (or such associated publications as *Venture Opinion*, which is strong on shell situations, and *New Issue Share Guide*) should be the sole source of guidance for a private investor. The serious national newspapers run occasional articles on penny shares, as do the main personal finance journals. *Money Observer* provides a portfolio of recommended stocks each year and its tipping record has been quite good. (Currently, it has 23 recommendations and/or notes on the main market, all priced at less than 20p.) One of the sensible points they all stress is that you should always give a broker specific instructions about the price you are prepared to pay for a share and what would satisfy you upon a sale. Do not leave things to chance or you may find the broker has paid an unnecessarily high price or got you the least attractive bargain on the day. You have to be as firm with your intermediary as you are with yourself.

Keeping your eyes and ears open

If you are going into penny stocks seriously, by all means invest in a subscription to a tip sheet, discounting in the process some of their colourful promotional literature. You must also be prepared to carry out research yourself and to monitor your investments closely when you have them. On the other hand, you must not take it all too seriously. You are not in it as a committed provider of capital to industry. You are dabbling in penny stocks for your own profit and to provide yourself with a little excitement and pleasure. You will have to be enthusiastic, but realistic; the sort of person who does not worry too much about the occasional setback. Do not pretend that you are other than a gambler, albeit a sensible and well informed one. And lastly, only play with money that can be lost without causing a family disaster.

Once you have decided to invest in lower-priced shares and in small companies, your programme will be determined by a combination of your financial resources and the time available to you. You can seek to follow inexpensive stocks generally, or choose a sector in which, in time, you will become something of a specialist. For example, you might like to take a special interest in investment trusts such as EFM Dragon Trust and First Charlotte Assets Trust, which are themselves 'pennies'.

In drawing up a list of companies to follow, your research will be facilitated by the new policy of the *Financial Times* of giving the market capitalisations of quoted companies in its Monday edition. This list spotlights the companies which are genuinely small. Once such information was very difficult for the private investor to obtain without access to sophisticated information facilities. Now all market capitalisations are laid out for you in tabulated form. The vast differences between public companies in their capitalisations makes fascinating reading. Perhaps you decide to restrict your investments to companies worth less than, say, £10 million. So how can you draw up your list of prospects?

You will not need a large sum of money to get involved and you could invest really modest amounts in equities of your choice. Dealing costs, however, make very small acquisitions uneconomic and I would suggest you do not spend less than £500 on any investment. Otherwise, the price will have to go a long way before you make any profit. Make sure, if you can, that you spread your money over a number of lower-priced shares but not so many that you cannot keep them under regular survey. Inexpensive, purpose-designed ledgers can be purchased in which there is space to record the progress of all investments. Do organise your affairs in this way as you will simply not be able to keep the information in your head.

Where do you go from here? You can gather information from a variety of sources. Even before you invest in a company, it is usually possible to acquire a copy of the company's latest 'Report and Accounts' by writing to the Company Secretary. When you invest and become part owner of the business you will be entitled to receive a copy of this annually, plus the six-month interim statement and, of course, any dividends. Read these carefully and file them. Annual General Meetings (AGM) can be brief and dull, but where possible do attend them. Take the opportunity of quizzing the directors and their advisers. It is the only day of the year they are on parade for you. Many small investors make a practice of tackling directors at AGMs and gleaning information or making judgements, which can be profitable. Do not be shy about tackling them from the floor of the meeting or over the cup of tea, coffee or something stronger which usually precedes an AGM. All such scraps of information are valuable.

Read all company communications carefully and, where you particularly oppose or endorse a proposed action by the board, cast your vote in general meeting or send in a proxy card beforehand. Even if you have had no previous experience of public companies, you will soon become accustomed to their jargon and style of presentation. Remember always that each report is an historic document by the time you receive it, a photographic record, as it were, of the company at a moment in time. Pay particular attention to the auditor's report, which is normally a formality confirming that the accounts present a true and fair view of the business activities and conform with the requirements of the various Companies Acts. If the auditors qualify their comments in any way it is a plain warning to investors to tread warily. In particular, read carefully any comment that a company's continuation as a going concern is dependent upon some factor or other. That normally suggests real trouble.

Do not expect the companies with inexpensive share prices to produce too many glossy brochures, videos or audio cassettes, as the giants often do. By their various sizes, or positions in the market, they usually do not have the money to spend on projecting themselves strongly. Be cautious when such companies engage in ambitious public relations efforts. It can indicate that the directors are doing something to project their image in the City (which might in time be good for you as an investor) but it could also indicate that the management's attention is straying from its main task, perhaps to make acquisitions with their inflated paper.

However, do not be too hasty in condemning, or being suspicious of, managements which appear to be chasing the headlines in the financial press. It *can* pay to be invested in a publicity-conscious company if the world accepts all the hype. At the same time remember that experience indicates that those concerns which benefit from an excess of column inches suffer out of all proportion when the going becomes rough. Sustained beating of the drum often helps in the short term with 'pennies' (if you are a seller) but do not invest simply because a firm appears to be always in the news, locally or in the trade or specialist press.

Above all, whether you act on advice in the tip sheets or the press generally, from a financial intermediary, a friend, or as the result of your own enquiries and research, remember that penny stocks will always comprise a unique corner of the investment scene. The classic considerations of price/earnings ratio and yields will mean nothing to you and your fellow investors. What will matter will be the potential of the firm in question – likely to be small and full of ideas, or large and struggling – but capable of being brought round again. The game is to catch such companies because they show promise or are likely to change dramatically. In all probability, you will be into and out of their shares long before they become much bigger or better established, at which time the market will view them more favourably using its traditional forms of analysis.

All comments so far have assumed you will be interested solely in British penny shares. In time, you might graduate into the vast US 'penny' field of some 30,000 stocks, or the roisterous Canadian and Australian markets. Modest information on these overseas 'pennies' is provided in the tip sheets from time to time. All those markets are intensely volatile. Big profits can be made but the problems of buying and selling are great and rogues abound.

In short, you must always be aware of the old marketing maxim of selling 'the sizzle and not the steak'. With 'pennies' you must make sure there is a reasonably good piece of steak on the grill. To obtain a good sniff of the sizzle, you will have to go into the kitchen as near as you can to the stove. And one thing to say in favour of the tipsters is that, whatever their shortcomings, they sometimes have access to the oven door!

5
WHY SMALL CAN BE BEAUTIFUL

It is not difficult to accept the premise that small and 'smaller' companies can operate more efficiently, and grow at a faster rate, than larger concerns. Experience of the 'minnows' in business normally shows them to be more go-ahead and with managements closely in touch with their suppliers, customers and staff. They are strongly motivated towards survival and expansion, with the directors often mortgaging their homes and possessions to keep them afloat during economic recessions. In time they often become highly prosperous and are regularly sold off to big companies with handsome capital gains.

The Hoare Govett Smaller Companies Index

Everyone involved in business has been aware for many years of the dynamism of smaller concerns and the fact that, growing from a lower base, they regularly expand at a faster rate than industrial and commercial giants. The performance of their shares in the markets has long been noted with admiration by both professionals and amateurs, but until 1987 it was not possible to measure just how well the 'minnows' performed in comparison with the market leaders. The statistical study which has transformed all our thinking, and proved that 'small can be beautiful' is known as the Hoare Govett Smaller Companies Index. The large stockbroking firm responsible for this important financial survey call it simply the 'HG–SC'.

This index is used primarily by other brokers and the major City institutions. Copies can be obtained by private investors, but sadly the annual subscription rate of £250 will probably be beyond most pockets. All you need to understand is the broad message which the HG–SC delivers to analysts faithfully each quarter – that smaller companies, on average, perform best of all. Upon this basis, the investor can create a portfolio of smaller quoted companies (which should do well) spiced with a selection of penny stocks (some of which just might do supremely well).

The message from the HG–SC has been taken on board by the City in the past year or so, but it is only slowly being translated into action by the institutions. The general caution can be explained in one word – research – or perhaps more accurately the lack of it. Only about 25 per cent of the companies defined by the Hoare Govett team as coming in the 'smaller' category have been
adequately researched. If detailed information is not available to the institutions, they will not invest.

The impact of the HG–SC Index has been considerable and no institution is nowadays without the latest report. It does not, however, spotlight individual companies but merely surveys the whole sector at the bottom of the various tiers of the stock market. The HG–SC comprises the lowest 10 per cent by capitalisation of the main UK equity shares. At the beginning of 1988, a total of 1236 companies were being surveyed. These represented three-quarters of all the equities listed in London.

The HG–SC, the only index of its kind, is produced by Hoare Govett in association with Elroy Dimson and Paul Marsh of the London Business School. Its files for 1987 chronicle clearly just how markedly the smaller companies out-performed the top 25 per cent of quoted firms in the closing months of the bull market. The HG–SC Index in that year out-performed the FT All Share Index by 13.2 per cent. A development of the index, known as the Extended HG–SC and which includes USM shares, beat the FT All Share by 13.4 per cent. The companies covered have market capitalisations of less than £100 million. The Extended version currently covers 1567 companies as against the 1236 in the basic index.

Although the index was launched in 1987, the statistics covered go back much further. It can be demonstrated that in the 33 years since 1955 the HG–SC with dividends re-invested, produced an annualised return of 20 per cent. This is a 6 per cent out-performance compared with the relative return of the FT All Share Index in the same period. Hoare Govett comment that the 'volatility of annual returns on the HG–SC has been similar to that of the FT All Share, indicating that an investment in a well spread portfolio of smaller companies is no riskier than a portfolio of larger stocks.'

The concept of 'smaller' companies being those with a market capitalisation of less than £100 million may seem odd at first reading. In fact, the HG–SC companies are very much smaller with an average capitalisation of just £27 million. This is near the level of 'under £10 million' or 'under £20 million' which various observers regard as being the areas of penny stocks. Such companies, however, are of relatively modest size in today's conditions when a house in a select part of London can be valued at £1 million.

Notwithstanding the market collapse in October the return on the HG–SC index, with all income re-invested, was about 21 per cent for 1987 as a whole, an impressive result. This compared with around 8 per cent for the FT All Share Index. The graph which appears on page 64 gives a graphic representation of the superiority of the smaller companies.

In the first nine months of 1988 the smaller companies continued to lead in the generally bearish conditions. In that period, the FT All Share rose by 12.3 per cent, whereas the HG–SC was up by 19.6 and the Extended HG–SC up by 19.1 per cent. However, there was an interesting development in the month of September alone which had significance for all investors. For the first time, in that month, the major companies out-performed the smaller. For that month the FT All Share was up 4.2 per cent against rises of 1.7 and 1.5 per cent respectively for the HG–SC and the Extended HG–SC.

Now what could have been the reason for this, and why was it significant? The answer seems to be that the big companies, the leaders of the pack, led the way down in 1987. Now, according to this theory, the fact that they out-performed the smaller fry in the month of September could well mean that they were also leading the way back to a bull market. In fact, the scenario may be as follows. The leaders went down first, then the smaller quoted companies and finally the penny shares. On the way back to bullish trading conditions, the positions may be: leaders first, smaller companies second and penny shares third. It is a reasonable scenario and takes account of the results of the HG–SC research. (In fact, the smaller companies went into the lead again in November and December, suggesting a delay in the return of a bull market. But there remained a strong belief among the small company watchers that the scenario quoted above would develop by mid-1989 – perhaps after substantial concessions to investors in the spring Budget.)

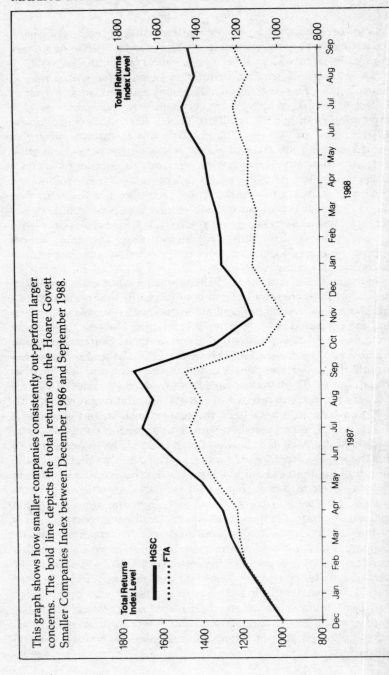

This graph shows how smaller companies consistently out-perform larger concerns. The bold line depicts the total returns on the Hoare Govett Smaller Companies Index between December 1986 and September 1988.

A broker specialising in the small company sector said this about penny stocks in particular:

'They went far too high before the crash and have in consequence behaved poorly since. But as the prices of the leaders and the smaller quoted companies resume a strong upward movement, there will be a trickle-down effect on the pennies. They will start rising again and, as in the past, fundamental considerations will not matter. But the key to their success will lie with the private investor who will have to become seriously interested in numbers once more. It may be some time before the institutions buy pennies again in quantity, as they were doing in 1987.'

Another pointer to the development of a bull market in 1989, is the great 'money mountain' currently held by the institutions. It was estimated in November 1988 that they had collectively in cash, or near-cash, more than £30 billion. It does not seem likely that this vast amount of cash can, or could, stay outside the market indefinitely, even with the attractions of high interest rates for those holding it. The effect of even a small part of this – say 10 per cent or £3 billion – being invested could be electrifying.

So it seemed in November 1988 that the 1987/88 bear market (which had lingered far longer than is customary with market downturns) was nearing its end. Market professionals were starting to feel mildly bullish and looking for the spark to light the flame again – with the privatisation of steel being one of the great hopes. Stock markets do traditionally over-react, in this country and around the world, and there were strong hopes in the last quarter of 1988 that the new year would see more optimistic conditions. After all, in the past 19 years, have we not seen six major market downturns and five spirited recoveries?

This does not rule out the possibility of a minor dip in the markets – perhaps for technical reasons – before an upswing comes in 1989. But come it will, and now is the time to plan to take advantage of it, both within the ranks of the smaller quoted and USM companies and among the perennially fascinating 'pennies'. At time of writing, most of these stocks are attractively priced and will generally look cheap a year from now. The British economy remains in good fettle despite the balance of payments problems brought about by our own affluence and the high interest rates. All that is required is a strong return to the markets by the cash-rich institutions, and a matching confidence by small investors, however much they were bruised by the events of Black Monday.

6

INVESTING THROUGH A UNIT TRUST

If you are a small investor, interested in the idea of penny shares and prepared to accept that small can be beautiful, then you have the option of investing directly yourself or reaching such companies via a unit trust or an investment trust. By using a collective vehicle, you may be forgoing the full benefit of a profit from time to time, but you will also be benefiting from the professional management of your money.

Background information

There are now well over 1200 unit trusts of which more than 70 invest solely in 'smaller' or 'emerging' companies. Most of these have penny shares within their portfolios. The proportion of penny shares varies enormously; some trusts had no 'pennies' under management at the time of writing, others reported they comprised up to 15 per cent of their portfolios, and various unit trusts spoke happily of having stocks which had once been 'pennies' but had since escalated in value. A few were secretive about penny holdings and this chapter is concerned with some 50 trusts which were prepared to expound upon their merits.

Unit trusts have been with us since the 1930s, so the idea is more than half a century old. They are much younger than their rival collective ventures, the investment trusts, whose origins date back to the 1860s. Unit trusts invest simply in shares on the stock market and, in a few cases, unlisted securities. When you buy units in a trust you are acquiring a stake in the shareholdings of that trust. All the shares held by a trust are valued regularly, usually each day, and the total is divided into units, each worth a fraction of the total value of the fund.

The cost of units is continually changing because it reflects the moving value of the whole portfolio. It is always possible to buy or to sell because the managers of each trust are able to buy back, or create, units to meet the demand. Unit trusts are popular with a sizeable minority of the British investing public because dealing is so simple, the risk is spread over a number of companies in a port-folio, and professional managers make all the decisions. The small investor may only have the resources to invest in two or three equities on the International Stock Exchange but with a unit trust holding he or she may have an indirect holding in a number of companies.

You make money from unit trusts through income paid out, usually twice a year, in the form of dividends and from growth in the sum you invested if you subsequently sell at a profit. Although many people have made handsome profits in the short term (often by getting into and out of unit trusts in their early days) they are essentially a long-term investment. And, as the companies are required to warn investors in all their promotional literature, the price of units can go down as well as up.

The reputation of unit trusts, sky high after the bull market years of the 1980s, suffered a big dent when share prices collapsed around the world in October 1987. Along with people holding direct stakes in quoted companies, the unit trust investors saw the value of their holdings slump overnight. Since then there has been a steady climb back in the prices of most units and seasoned investors have regained their confidence. But others have liqui-dated their holdings and returned to safer, if less potentially profit-able, forms of investment.

One can understand the concern felt by those who had been in unit trusts only a short time when Black Monday wreaked its havoc. The figures tell the story simply and starkly. At the time, the total value of funds under management by the authorised unit trusts was a record £50,333 million. The stock market collapse forced this total down to £34,568 million in November. Through-out 1988 there was a recovery in the value of funds under manage-ment, partly because share prices had risen and partly because new funds had been launched. By the start of November 1988 the 153 companies reporting to the Unit Trust Association were man-aging combined assets worth £41,271 million.

At that time the number of unitholder accounts stood at

4,934,000, against the peak of 5,080,000 achieved in January 1988. (Curiously, there were fewer accounts – 4,930,000 – just before the crash.) This figure, however, is not a totally reliable guide to investor feeling about unit trusts because many people during 1988 disposed of units with disappointing performances and purchased again. Also, the number of authorised unit trusts has continued to rise – from 1106 in October 1987 to 1230 just 12 months later.

For all the success of the unit trust movement in recent years, it has a long way to go before it can boast an army of investors to rival that of the building societies, or of the nine million people who currently hold shares quoted on the International Stock Exchange. Nobody knows precisely how many people are unit trust investors. The Unit Trust Association guesses that the total is up to 1,500,000 but some estimates are lower, while others suggest the figure may be around 1,750,000. Investors are said to hold at least three or four unit trusts each. However, this is not a vast total when compared to the eight million or so people who have more than £5000 invested in a building society.

Unit trusts are certainly the simplest way for a person of modest capital to invest in the stock market and, with all the money spent on their promotion in recent years, it is curious that they have not achieved a larger share. The crash was certainly a setback to the movement and has caused some people to return to the building society fold. Many of these left the unit trust ranks not just because prices had fallen but because they were concerned about the confusion and inefficiency within some management groups in the wake of the stock market problems. So should the investor interested in penny shares and smaller companies ignore the unit trusts and wait for better times? The answer must be a firm 'no'.

The would-be investor in unit trusts is well advised to consider not only the large number of people with capital who have shunned such investments in the past but the considerable minority (at least 1,500,000 strong) who have made excellent profits over the years and remain intensely loyal.

The loyalty of experienced unit trust investors was confirmed by a major survey reported in September 1988 by Gartmore Fund Managers, one of the leading management groups. It sent a questionnaire to its 105,000 unitholders, of whom more than 10,000 replied. The answers, analysed by an independent research company, showed continuing investor confidence in the unit trust concept. More than half (55 per cent) planned to leave their investments unchanged for the next six months while only 1 per cent said they intended to fully liquidate their holdings.

A quarter of the investors in this large sample said they were planning to rebalance their portfolios by switching into other trusts, while 22 per cent indicated they would be buying more units. (The figures add up to more than 100 per cent because some people answered questions in more than one category.) Overall, the findings of the survey indicated that a significant number of ordinary investors were satisfied with unit trusts as long-term investments.

Smaller companies unit trusts

For the unit trusts invested in smaller and emerging companies, 1988 has been a year of mixed fortunes. Broadly, their investments have under-performed the market as a whole. The shares of the smaller listed (and unlisted) companies have been more difficult to market and prices have fallen steeply when there has been any selling pressure. It is the shares of the major blue-chip companies which have led the climb back to pre-Black Monday levels.

For the future, however, the smaller company unit trusts are widely regarded as having first class potential for growth. There have been plenty of bargains around in 1988 and far-sighted fund managers have been buying shrewdly. They are bullish about the next few years, pointing to the rapid growth of many such firms, their attractive yields, and the possibilities for expansion which lie ahead, especially for British 'tiddlers' in Europe. Although no one rules out the possibility of further stock market dips or 'corrections', the general feeling is that well chosen investments outside the big leagues will do better than the big names in the last months of this decade and the early 1990s.

John Ainsworth, Fund Manager of the Capital House Smaller Companies Trust, explained the bright prospects of the sector in these words:

It is now generally accepted that over the medium to long-term small companies provide better returns than large companies. In simple terms this is because it is easier to grow faster from a small base. Small companies are normally much less diversified than their larger counterparts, which enables them to exploit niche markets whilst being flexible enough to adapt quickly to changes in market trends.

Small companies are currently out of favour with the stock market. In many cases this has resulted in share price valuations at a significant discount to the market at a time when earnings are forecast to grow well in excess of the corporate average.

Given that growth in corporate earnings are forecast to slow markedly in 1989 it is only a question of time before the value of smaller companies is more widely accepted.

One consequence of the crash has been that fund managers have accepted the need for more serious research in the smaller company field. The same applies to private investors. The days of picking penny shares by running down the columns of the *Financial Times* must be over.

How much will it cost?

If you decide that all, or part, of your exposure to penny shares and smaller company shares will be through unit trusts the outlay can be very modest indeed. You can either invest a lump sum or pay so much each month to build up a holding. If you are prepared to make a lump sum investment, the minimum can be as low as £100 although most companies seek at least £250, £500 or £1000, with smaller minimums for further stakes.

Virtually all unit trust companies offer savings schemes where the minimum (in the case of the Midland Bank and a few others) can be as low as £10 per month. More common minimums are £20, £25 and £30 per month. Such a payment buys units at whatever the offer price is at the time. You are thus accumulating capital in a painless way at average prices, your monthly payment purchasing more units when prices are low and less when they are high. In a depressed market a savings scheme can be a good thing for a new investor and many long-term savers have prospered in the wake of Black Monday.

Normally you can stop a savings scheme at any time and cash in the units you have accumulated, but do make sure this facility is available to you when you choose to invest with a unit trust company. Generally speaking, a savings scheme is the simplest and safest way into unit trust investment. Your decision is, first, which one of the 15 recognised sectors interests you, and then the specific unit trust. The Unit Trust Association will provide you with information on unit trust companies and explain its system of sectors.

Who buys unit trusts?

What sort of club would you be joining? At present, unit trust investors appear to be primarily male although the ranks of women investors, especially in the younger age groups, are growing apace. The previously mentioned substantial Gartmore research indicated that the sex ratio was 85 men to 15 women of whom 15 per cent were under 40, 15 per cent between 40 and 50, and 61 per cent 50 or over. Women accounted for 20 per cent of the investors under the age of 30.

Nearly eight out of ten (77 per cent) of the respondents said they also owned shares, while 86 per cent had building society accounts. Some 15 per cent of the investors had most of their money in a building society, whereas 35 per cent invested mainly in unit trusts, another 9 per cent put most of their money into shares. So you can see that most of the other members of the club have decided to spread their risks widely, as you should.

Similarly, it makes sense not to have all your eggs in one unit trust basket. The Gartmore research confirmed this and showed that only 7 per cent of their investors dealt solely with them. A total of 44 per cent used between two and five investment groups and 45 per cent invested with six or more groups. Just over half (51 per cent) dealt directly with Gartmore, while 38 per cent used a financial adviser and 8 per cent used both channels of investment. (The figures above do not necessarily add up to 100 per cent because of the way the questionnaire was framed.)

How secure are they?

How secure are you nowadays in acquiring unit trusts via a professional intermediary? Within the framework of the Financial Services Act, most unit trust companies have laid down new terms of business to be observed by intermediaries selling their products. A standard form of such an agreement, proposed by the Unit Trust Association, requires the following points to be satisfied:

1. That the intermediary is properly authorised by one of the self-regulatory bodies.
2. That the status of the client is made clear. Business gained as a result of a cold-call by an intermediary, for example, requires the unit trust manager to provide a cooling-off period.
3. That proper disclosure of commission is made at the point of sale. (The intermediary must either say he is being paid the standard rate laid down by the Life Assurance and Unit Trust Regulatory Organisation, or disclose the actual figure.)
4. That the investor is offered the relevant disclosure documents (including the most recent manager's report for the unit trust in question and full particulars of the scheme) before a deal is concluded.
5. That arrangements for prompt settlement exist.

Most unit trust companies are understood to have adopted terms of business along the above lines. While it is assumed that readers of this book will tend to make their own decisions and will not purchase a unit trust in response to a cold-call, it is reassuring to know that, should you decide to invest in response to an approach by a salesman, there is a cooling-off period. This works as follows. After such a sale (by an independent or a tied agent) the unit trust company has to send out a contract note within 24 hours and a cancellation notice inside seven days. From receipt of the cancellation notice, investors have 14 days to withdraw from the contract. In that event they get back the 'offer' price of the unit trusts prevailing on the day the cancellation notice is received, but subject to a maximum of the original amount invested.

The investor who has initially responded to a cold-call approach thus loses money if the price of the unit trust falls within the cancellation period. However, he or she does not have to pay the initial charges of the unit trust company which are nowadays around 6 per cent. If the unit trust company does not get the cancellation notice to the investor within the prescribed period then it bears any losses on the transaction.

As might be expected, there is no cooling-off period if you initiate the investment yourself, if you give instructions to a broker or intermediary, or you clip a coupon from a newspaper and are thus under no pressure to invest. (In the latter case, only an improperly worded advertisement can give you cause to seek a refund of your money.) Protection is also forfeited if you enter into a client agreement with a broker, whereby you clearly have solicited professional help and advice. To sum up, the sensible new rules are designed to protect the small investor from high pressure selling but are not a means of escaping from a contract if you have second thoughts or a unit price slumps.

Assuming you take the initiative yourself and do not wait for a salesman to knock on your door to sell units (which is now possible) you can purchase direct, perhaps 'off the page', or through an intermediary, a bank, or even nowadays in the office of a building society. (The Cheltenham & Gloucester have announced that they are now prepared to sell units in any UK authorised fund across their counters.) The Society said its research indicated that 'nearly a quarter' of people questioned favoured buying from a building society if possible. No advice is given and it is an 'execution only' service.

Monitoring your investment

Once you have invested you can follow the progress of your units in the columns of the *Financial Times* and other quality news-papers. To calculate how much your investment is worth simply multiply the number of units you own (shown on the contract note) by the bid price. For a comparison of various funds, you can check the performance tables published in various personal finance magazines (notably *Money Management* and *Planned Savings*) and occasionally reviewed in the newspapers. Statistics are also published by the Unit Trust Association and the managers of the funds in which you invest will send you a report twice a year.

You will see two prices quoted for unit trusts – the 'bid' (which is what investors receive when they sell) and the 'offer' (the figure at which they can buy the units). The difference between the two is called the 'spread' which is usually around 6 per cent but under the Securities and Investments Board rules can occasionally be as wide as 11 per cent. Before you make any profit on your units, the price you paid must rise by more than the amount of the 'spread' to catch up with the selling price. The managers, of course, cover their costs and make their profits on the 'spread'.

Pricing is a complicated matter. Unit trust managers can value on an 'historic' basis, ie yesterday's asset values. Under this scheme you can deal at the price you see quoted in the morning newspapers. The newer concept is 'forward pricing' which means the price is the next regular valuation after you deal. You therefore have to wait a time to know the actual price at which you bought or sold. Some managers use both systems, depending on the time of day your order goes through and the price may vary from morning to afternoon. Remember though, in the new investment climate you have the right to insist on forward pricing if you wish, regardless of the company's normal policy.

Unit trusts differ too as to when they value. Some do it first thing in the morning, some at midday, others in the afternoon. In certain cases, valuation takes place weekly, or even once a fort-night. With some of the largest management groups, the valu-ations take place several times a day. In time, thanks to modern technology, some companies may even be on 'real time' pricing, providing an up-to-the minute valuation for every transaction. When the time comes to sell, you will become aware of a 'cancel-lation' price. This is the bottom figure allowed by the SIB for the re-purchase of units. The bid price almost invariably rules but, when there is a great deal of selling, you might have to be content with the cancellation price. It is instructive to check both prices. If the bid and cancellation figures are close, or identical, it means that a good deal of selling is taking place.

When a new trust is launched, a discount (normally in the 1 to 3 per cent range) is often offered. Sometimes special discounts are offered to tempt existing shareholders to increase their holdings. Such discounts can be attractive but do not let them interfere with your own buying plans or influence your investment policy. Once you have bought, the company should send you a contract note within 24 hours detailing the unit price, cancellation price, the number of units purchased, the initial charge and the amount paid. Within three weeks your registration certificate should arrive. Keep both documents carefully as proof of ownership because they will be required by the Inland Revenue and when you eventually sell the units. To sell, endorse the unit certificate and send it back to the fund manager. The proceeds of the sale should arrive within five days.

Of the unit trusts which invest in smaller, or 'emerging' companies, only one nowadays mentions 'penny share' in its title. This is the Penny Share Fund of the Edinburgh-based Waverley Asset Management. The group manages some £30 million worth of assets of which about £2 million is in the 'penny' unit trust. These investments are made in companies based all over the world.

Waverley's limit is 100p. Enquiries revealed that of their holdings, 19 of the 51 companies came within the arbitrary definition of 50p and below. If you are seeking statistical encouragement for investing in penny shares on an international basis, then Waverley can oblige. In the first nine months of the trust's history – from 2 November 1987 until 31 August 1988 – the price, on an offer to offer basis, rose by 18.2 per cent. During the same period, the FT All-Share Index by 4 per cent, and the FTSE 100 by 1.7 per cent.

The great proportion of unit trusts invested in smaller companies cover UK equities. They represent perhaps two-thirds of the total. Most go all out for growth, which is understandable in this sector. There are a few, however, which seek to specialise in providing a good income. Such a trust is the Henderson Smaller Companies Dividend (managing £43 million of assets). A small proportion are in the penny share category but are viewed as being good prospects for producing rising dividends. The price of this trust increased 278.7 per cent in the five years to August 1988 but was then 10 per cent below its level of a year earlier.

Unit trusts to choose from

In all, I looked at 50 unit trusts invested in smaller companies in the UK and overseas. The majority are confined to this country and seek capital growth. The UK trusts are itemised below to indicate the variety available. Fuller details should be sought from the fund managers concerned, or from a professional intermediary. The figure quoted in brackets in each case is the approximate value of the assets under management within the fund at the time this book was written. The trusts shown are in alphabetical order.

Allied Dunbar Smaller Companies Trust (£27.5 million) aspires to 'considerable capital and income performance'. About 5 per cent of the holdings are penny shares. The managers do not see any significant correlation between penny shares and performance unless other criteria exist such as market capitalisation and earnings growth rate.

Allied Dunbar Second Smaller Companies Trust (£24.3 million) has a far greater sprinkling of penny share investments with 15 per cent of the holdings priced at 50p or less. But again the managers state that what is important to them is not the low price but the number of shares in issue and the earnings.

Barings First Smaller Companies (£34.6 million) is invested primarily in UK companies although some overseas investments which appear to have the potential for above average growth may be included from time to time. Eight per cent of the portfolio is in 'pennies' which the managers say can achieve 'significant performance', although marketability of such shares may occasionally present problems.

Buckmaster Emerging Growth Fund (£10.16 million) pins its faith in what it calls 'up and coming' UK companies. These are seen as being companies 'still small enough to command above average flexibility and speed of manoeuvre but already large enough to compete with major participants in their chosen markets'.

Buckmaster Smaller Companies Fund (£12 million) defines smaller UK companies as those with a market capitalisation of less than £120 million. Policy is to visit the companies, and meet the management, before investing. There are no 'pennies' in the portfolio.

Dimensional UK Small Companies Trust (£86.3 million) has a diversified portfolio of small listed British companies. Capital growth is the aim and no attention is given to income considerations. Of 700 stocks some 100 were penny shares by my definition. The managers are, however, small company devotees regardless of whether the price is below 50p.

Framlington Capital Trust (£122 million) is a larger and older trust, the price of which had shown a 340.7 per cent increase in the seven years to July 1988. This trust is invested mainly in smaller companies. Of 239 investments some 11 were 'pennies'.

Framlington Smaller Companies (£8.5 million) seeks capital growth in the medium to long-term and looks at companies with market capitalisations of less than £150 million. 'Pennies' are scarce in the portfolio – there was just one at the time of my check. This trust made its debut in November 1987 after the crash and the price has moved well since.

Gartmore UK Smaller Companies Recovery (£22.2 million) seeks growth rather than income, but the managers assert the yield is still 'likely to be in line with that of the FT Index'. Penny shares account for 8 per cent of the portfolio. Growth over five years to August 1988 was 236.7 per cent.

Granville Small Companies Fund (£1.7 million) has a different idea of 'small' to some similar funds, investing in UK companies capitalised up to, and around, £50 million. Granville specialises in the affairs of small and medium-sized companies, their employees and shareholders, so setting up such a unit trust was a natural development. Of perhaps 30 holdings no more than one or two are 'pennies'. Price growth in the two and a quarter years since formation in May 1986 was 48.4 per cent.

Hambros Smaller Companies Trust (£31.2 million) invests in companies with 'relatively small capitalisations'. Research revealed that some 5.7 per cent of the portfolio represented penny stocks.

Holborn Small Companies Trust (£113 million) is managed by the Prudential Holborn unit trust team. It is primarily linked to UK investments but up to 20 per cent of the portfolio may be in overseas equities. Although the majority of the companies will be quoted, the trust can invest up to 25 per cent in USM stocks, including up to 5 per cent in unquoted vehicles. Approximately 2 per cent were priced at 50p or less.

Lazard Small Companies Growth Trust (£11.6 million) targets companies with market capitalisations below £120 million and sound growth prospects. The managers, in commenting on penny shares, observe that prices 'rise to reflect the growth in a company's profits and earnings per share which are influenced by any nuber of factors. Shares are selected therefore on their relative value and not their absolute value.' Price of the trust had risen 182.6 per cent in five years.

M & G Smaller Companies Fund (£95.8 million) has chalked up an impressive record since September 1967. Growth in those 21 years has been 3478.6 per cent for the accumulation units with net income reinvested. The annual compound growth rate has been 18.7 per cent. A proportion of this fund is invested in the USM and unquoted securities.

MLA UK Smaller Companies (£7 million) tries to identify the 'blue chips of tomorrow'. The managers state that 'research shows that smaller companies with proven entrepreneurial spirit are likely to out-perform large corporations in terms of capital growth for some time to come'. The current prices of such companies often fail to reflect their actual prospects.

Manulife Smaller Companies (Manufacturers Life, £25 million) could boast a healthy increase in the value of its units in mid-1988 compared with the general drop in UK equity indices since the crash. It claimed this stemmed from a philosophy of concentrating on 'lowly rated, often under-researched stocks'. Of the holdings 5 per cent tend to be in 'pennies' although the managers say that such shares can be over-valued and dull performers.

The **Midland Smaller Companies Unit Trust** (£28.5 million) sees 'smaller' as being a company with a market capitalisation below £100 million. Such concerns are considered to have the ability to 'grow faster than large companies with no greater risk'. Factors considered are dynamic management, niche products and services, technology leads, and tiny but expandable market shares; 2 per cent of the fund was in shares priced below 50p.

MIM Britannia Smaller Companies (£18 million) aims to provide a combination of capital growth with an average income. The portfolio may include, from time to time, a small number of USM stocks. A search disclosed just one penny share. Over the eight years to the end of June 1988 the price increased 568.2 per cent.

The **Geoffrey Morley Smaller Companies Trust** (£17 million) is one of those defining small as £100 million capitalisation or less. There are no penny shares in this portfolio, the managers believing that companies with proven records have gone beyond the 50p tag.

The **Murray Smaller Companies Fund** is managed by Murray Johnstone Unit Trust Management of Glasgow and can point to above average performance in both the short and the long term. The managers have the same attitude towards penny shares as at Geoffrey Morley, and lay stress on strong management, a proven track record, and a clear strategy for business growth. On an offer-to-bid basis, with net income re-invested, in the five year period to July 1988 the price of this unit trust increased by 230.8 per cent.

New Court Smaller Companies Fund (£21.7 million) is one of a 'small is beautiful' quartet of trusts under the control of Rothschild Asset Management. Growth with a 'reasonable income' as the object. The criterion is 'less than £100 million' capitalisation.

Royal Life UK Emerging Companies Trust (£9.8 million) promises investors it will go for 'all out capital growth'. Enquiries showed 8.5 per cent of the fund was invested in penny shares. This is a post-crash vehicle, launched in February 1988.

The **N M Schroder Smaller Companies Fund** (£42.2 million) similarly regards income as of secondary importance and is concerned solely with above average growth. No penny shares are currently included in the portfolio.

Scottish Mutual UK Smaller Companies Equity (£114.5 million) takes a different approach to many in the sector, targeting the 'securities of companies outside the top 100 by market capitalisation'. But there is still room for a few 'pennies' – 3.8 per cent at the time of survey. The increase in price over a three-year period was 132.5 per cent.

Sentinel Small Companies Fund (£14 million) has holdings in OTC stocks and 7 per cent of the fund was invested in penny shares. Normally the company chosen for investment will have a market capitalisation of below £100 million, but sometimes stakes are taken in larger concerns to provide liquidity.

TR Smaller Companies (£29 million, managed by Touche Remnant Unit Trust Management) advised that 10 of the 90 stocks in the portfolio could be defined as penny shares. Their total value constituted 7.7 per cent of the fund. The units were first issued at 25p in January 1984 and in August 1988 the price was in the 95p–101p range, a recovery from the post-crash low of 69–74p.

TSB Smaller Companies Unit Trust (£12 million) looks for companies with high growth potential. The managers had two penny stocks in their portfolio which had given an 'above average performance'. In addition there were five stocks which had been purchased at below 50p but had since risen substantially above that level. The launch period of this trust straddled the stock market collapse. Nine months later the price had risen by just over 20 per cent.

Windsor Smaller Companies Trust (£3.1 million) is interested, generally, in companies with capitalisations below £50 million; but it will also look at those up to £150 million. A high proportion – 15 per cent – comprised penny shares and the managers advised that they had 'performed at least as well as the fund in general'. Launched in November 1987, it has been a consistently good performer since.

If you are interested in placing your money in smaller companies on a world-wide basis, then there are international unit trusts available. The largest is the **Holborn International Small Companies Trust** (Prudential Holborn, £204 million) which invests in equities of companies with 'relatively small' market capitalisations. Specifically excluded are leading firms in Britain, the USA and Japan. Approximately 3.5 per cent of the investments were penny shares.

Another international trust looks to 'emerging' companies for growth. This is the **Perpetual International Emerging Companies Fund** (Perpetual £17 million) where the emphasis is on smaller companies, new industries and businesses which have recently been involved in takeovers, mergers, or public flotations. Perpetual have an enviable record in the growth line and manage in all £400 million worth of assets from their base in Henley-upon-Thames, Oxfordshire. Part of the Emerging Companies Fund (6 per cent at time of writing) is invested in penny shares. Both the Holborn and the Perpetual international trusts have recovered well during 1988.

Let us now look at three unit trusts invested in the smaller companies of Western Europe. Two have almost the same amount of assets under management. The **Henderson European Smaller Companies** (Henderson £35 million) is restricted to companies whose market capitalisation at time of purchase is £60 million or less. Occasionally, this rule is broken if the company is larger but the 'float' is restricted. Holdings tend to be held on a long-term basis and portfolio turnover is relatively low. There are no 'pennies' here because most European shares are much 'heavier' than their UK counterparts. This trust had a difficult time after the crash when massive redemptions led to forced sales, but the position had been stabilised by the second half of 1988.

The **New Court Smaller European Companies** is one of four specialist funds managed by N M Rothschild Asset Management, part of a group managing some £7 billion. The European unit trust assets are around £36 million. The Rothschild definition of 'smaller' is a market capitalisation of less than £100 million.

A smaller fund in the same field is the **MIM Britannia European Smaller Companies** (MIM Britannia £10.5 million) where once again no 'pennies' are held in the portfolio.

There is similarly a good choice of trusts invested in Japan, which has produced sparkling growth performance for many investors but has more recently had periods in the doldrums. Again, market conditions rule out the possibility of having what we define as penny shares in the various portfolios. The objectives of three typical trusts are similar. They are the **MIM Britannia Japan Smaller Companies** (£17 million), **EFM Smaller Japanese Companies** (£6 million) and **Dunedin Japan Smaller Companies** (Dunedin Fund Managers). Of the three, the Dunedin managers tend to seek the real 'tiddlers' on the Second Section and OTC markets. This approach seems to be paying off as the Dunedin fund has been hovering near the top of its sector of late.

M & G, a giant in the unit trust movement, has its **Japan Smaller Companies Fund** (£17.8 million) which includes some shares quoted only on the OTC market in Tokyo. All aspects of the Japanese economy are covered, including new technologies and 'emerging' businesses. The accumulation units had increased in value by 139.6 per cent in the four years from launch to August 1988.

If the Pacific region excites you as a long term prospect, then you can gain access to smaller Australian companies via the **New Court Smaller Australasian Companies Fund**. (The term 'Australasia', of course, embraces New Zealand as well.) The size of this fund is almost £11 million and its price has recovered in an encouraging manner since the stock market collapse.

A much wider choice is available if you decide to try the vast number of small companies within the North American markets. Six trusts were surveyed before writing this book, with funds under management ranging from just £2 million to more than £25 million. In this sector it must be noted that the definition of 'smaller' may cover companies with market capitalisation as high as $500 million.

The **Framlington American Smaller Companies** (£25 million) is the largest in this field. Its managers put their faith in companies regarded as being 'turnaround' situations. Few are 'pennies'; when I enquired, four of the 149 shares held were valued at less than the equivalent of 50p. Next largest in terms of assets under management is the **MIM Britannia US Smaller Companies Trust** (nearly £18 million). Henderson's **American Smaller Companies Trust** (£11.5 million) searches for shares with 'above average earnings growth potential' from a smaller market capitalisation base. The price of the Henderson fund has improved particularly well during 1988.

Another good performer in 1988 has been the **M & G American Smaller Companies Fund** (£21.7 million assets under management) which invests in both the USA and Canada. At the time of writing, the managers were talking of the future of smaller companies in North America as being 'very positive'.

There is the opportunity of participating in the Canadian economy via the **New Court Smaller Canadian Companies Fund** (£11.9 million). As with the similar European and Australasian funds, you can only buy accumulation units, ie there is no distribution of income. The **Mercury American Smaller Companies Fund** (Mercury Fund Managers, £7 million) offers both distribution and accumulation units. Income is not, generally, a big consideration. Some Canadian shares may be held. The smallest fund in the group surveyed is the **F & C US Smaller Companies** (£2 million) where investments are made in 'smaller and medium-sized' North American equities.

Finally, for unit trust investors who would like to make the world their oyster, Schroder Investment Management offer the **SIM Overseas Smaller Companies Fund** (£142.8 million) which seeks capital growth solely through smaller companies operating outside the UK.

7

INVESTMENT TRUSTS CAN HELP

There are more than 30 investment trusts which hold stakes in smaller and emerging companies or invest in what we call 'penny shares'. As with unit trusts, it can make sense for the private investor to test the 'small is beautiful' theory by including a few such trusts in his or her portfolio. There is a wide choice available and, almost invariably, there will be 'pennies' among their investments.

You can invest in investment trusts which concentrate purely on smaller enterprises, in Britain or abroad, or on a world-wide basis. You can choose a trust which looks for 'emerging' companies likely to be seeking a full listing in the next few years. 'Special situations' is another area, and here the managers will be looking at firms where a takeover may be in prospect, or a management buyout is likely. There are sectors, too (as with unit trusts), such as the USA, Europe or Property.

There is evidence that investment trusts have emerged in good shape from the confusion which followed the international stock market crash in October 1987. After being in the comparative doldrums for some years, during which unit trusts secured a pre-eminent position, they are once again being promoted actively in the market-place. Strenuous attempts are being made to stress the long-term attraction of this old-fashioned form of investing. A favourite promotional statistic is that £1000 staked in investment trusts after the war, on 31 December 1945, would have been worth £166,425 on 31 December 1987 – after the stock market crash.

What are investment trusts?

The investor contemplating a stake in an investment trust must appreciate, above all, that it is a company, like any other public limited company. Unlike public companies, however, they do not manufacture a product or provide a service. Their role is limited to investing in other companies (quoted and unquoted) in the UK and abroad, managing those investments for their shareholders. The shares of investment trust companies are acquired, and disposed of, through the stock market.

Investment trusts are subject to the same legislation as all other public limited companies, and submit to the same regulations of the International Stock Exchange. These market requirements relate chiefly to the necessary disclosure of information to maintain a proper market in the shares. Investment trusts are not, as such, covered by the new Financial Services Act, by the regulations of the Securities and Investments Board, or any of its regulatory bodies. Their managers are, however, fully subject to the regulatory system.

Strictly speaking, investment trusts are not 'trusts' at all. The word 'trust' was used to describe them in their Victorian infancy and the name has remained with us. An early court decision (later overturned) held that they were not legal trusts so the companies already in the field converted themselves into limited companies to place the issue beyond doubt.

It is now 120 years since this co-operative investment product was first offered to the small investor. Foreign & Colonial (still in the business) set up the first in 1868 with the laudable aim of giving the 'investor of moderate means the same advantage as the large capitalist in diminishing the risk of investing in Foreign and Colonial Government stocks by spreading the investment over a number of different stocks'. That definition still holds good today, although equities have largely supplanted government securities in the portfolios of the investment trusts.

Investment trusts flourished in the 1880s during international boom conditions but the next decade saw some casualties in their ranks. By 1900 the investor had a choice of more than 100 and, of the companies which are members today of the Association of Investment Trust Companies (AITC) nearly one-quarter were in existence at the start of the twentieth century. They survived during the years which followed the Wall Street crash of 1929 and retained a strong public following until the mid-1960s, by which time their money was usually going into equities rather than fixed interest securities.

The last quarter century has been one of fluctuating fortunes for the investment trusts. They became less attractive to the private investor as building societies, insurance companies and unit trust promoters moved to the centre of the investment stage. Encouraged by tax concessions, people increasingly used their savings to invest in private property, pension schemes and a variety of new financial products. The investment trusts retaliated by wooing the big City institutions who respected the expertise of the trust managers and quickly became their major investors.

There were attempts in the 1960s and 1970s to win back the interest of small investors, notably through the introduction of split capital investment trusts. Such trusts have both capital and income shares. Capital growth is attributed to one type of share, the flow of dividends to the other. This innovation had some appeal but did not arrest the general decline of interest among private investors.

Throughout this period, investment trusts had a very difficult time and there were some who forecast that they might disappear altogether one day. The shares of the trusts fell out of favour and prices were marked down sharply. It became commonplace for shares to change hands at prices well below the value of their underlying investments. 'Discount to net asset value' became a major consideration for purchasers of trust shares; discounts of 30 to 40 per cent were typical in the mid and late 1970s.

The period of large discounts gave the investment trusts a poor image and many readers will recall critical articles in the press a decade ago and less. A major consequence of the steep discount era was that City institutions hit the takeover trail in search of assets 'on the cheap'. Many old-established trusts were swallowed up in that way, or were merged with other trusts. The best interests of private investors were not always served in such transactions.

The investment trusts hit back in various ways, one device being to adopt the unitisation course, or the conversion of their companies into unit trusts. In such cases, investment trusts are wound up and the investors are offered in units the approximate net asset value of their shares. Units are then issued in a new, or an existing, unit trust. This process of unitising is still continuing. In more recent years too, the investment trust companies have fought back against their big predators by appealing again to the public, first through specialist investment trusts (such as those covered in this chapter) and, more recently, through savings schemes.

But, compounding the problems of the trusts, the institutions which had been their saviours in the early post-war decades, buying the expertise of their fund managers, embarked upon building up in-house investment teams. Their holdings in investment trusts often came to be regarded as a burden and share prices remained depressed as a result. This situation is still with us, though the threat to trust share prices is not as severe as it was in the 1970s.

At the beginning of this decade, investment trusts seemed to have few close supporters in the financial world or in the press. But the bull market which raged through the 1980s brought renewed interest in the trusts and in recent years the movement itself has become far more aggressive and enterprising. The corporate image has been given a vigorous polish and the claims of the once all-conquering unit trust companies have been challenged. Annual accounts and statements are far clearer than they were and more detailed and meaningful information is being given to the public on investments held.

Above all, as with unit trusts, there has been the big move towards specialisation, both industrially and geographically. No longer do the vast general trusts dominate the scene. The names of numerous trusts have been changed to stress the fresh approach. The historic decline in the number of trusts has continued, but the increase in value of the remaining trusts has more than compensated. In all this activity, the managers have sought to find new ways of growth, and in the process have looked with more favour than previously on the 'pennies' and the small companies.

Investment trusts today

Today there are roughly 200 investment trusts in existence, managing between them at least £21 billion worth of assets. Of these, 161 are members of the Association of Investment Trust Companies. The AITC speaks for around 80 per cent of the trusts, but 95 per cent of the value of the assets under management. The individual totals under management range from under £2 million to more than £1 billion.

Before the crash, total assets of AITC members exceeded £26 billion. This figure fell to around £19 billion before a recovery started which has run through much of 1988. The latest assets figure of £21 billion plus is not simply a reflection of share prices. It also covers the fact that various trusts have disappeared through unitisation and reorganisation while several new ones have started, albeit on a small scale. Discounts, which widened to an average of about 20 per cent in the last quarter of 1987, had improved to 17 per cent at time of writing.

The discount can be viewed either pessimistically or optimistically by the private investor. On the one hand, it may be depressing to note that the price of an investment trust share is usually below the value of its underlying assets. This results from the simple working of the law of supply and demand in the stock market. On the other hand, the discount enables the investor to acquire more assets and dividends with his or her money. If the assets behind a trust are worth, say, 100p and the price is 80p, the discount of 20 per cent means you are buying on a 'bonus' basis.

Shareholders in an investment trust can make money in two ways: through an increase in the value of the underlying investments, and through a narrowing of the discount, ie its reduction from, say, 20 per cent to 10 per cent. These twin advantages do not apply to investments in unit trusts. Sometimes, too, the price of a trust rises above its net asset value and when this happens the shares are said to be trading at a premium.

The AITC performs nowadays with a vigour and a high profile which would have seemed impossible a few years ago. Its main concern for a long time has been that intermediaries have been reluctant to advise clients to put money into investment trusts because there was only meagre commission in it for them. The Association's case has been that there must be a move towards a fee-paying industry as one way of ensuring that advice is impartial and independent. In August 1988 it won a significant victory when FIMBRA, in issuing new *Guidelines on Best Advice*, acknowledged that investment trusts must be among the products to be considered by intermediaries.

The introduction of savings schemes (which played so important a part in the development of unit trusts) is now doing the same for investment trusts. All the major trusts within the AITC today offer a savings scheme facility for the purchase of shares and an increasing number provide a selling facility with a variety of scale charges.

Research carried out by AITC well after the 1987 crash is relevant. The main findings of this study were that 60 per cent of the large sample interviewed and 83 per cent of those using investment trust savings schemes had invested without taking advice from anyone.

Of the people covered in the AITC survey, 42 per cent were first time buyers of investment trusts. Two-thirds of the new investors reported having less than £50,000 free capital available for investment, indicating a level of prosperity but not great wealth. Most learned about investment trusts from a newspaper (37 per cent), a specialist financial publication (21 per cent) or an advertisement (7 per cent). Professional advisers or stockbrokers accounted for only 19 per cent.

Of the minority who did take advice before purchasing their investment trusts, 18 per cent had consulted a stockbroker and 4 per cent another financial adviser, 3 per cent an accountant and 2 per cent a bank manager. These figures for the professionals were overshadowed by the proportion of investment trust investors who had relied on friends or relatives for guidance (13 per cent).

The profile of investment trust investors indicates that their average age is coming down. Savings schemes have obviously contributed largely to this – 57 per cent of investors under the age of 45 were using schemes to build up holdings. Of the agents used to acquire investment trusts, 38 per cent were via savings schemes, ie through the companies themselves, using 'wholesalers rather than retailers', in the jargon of the industry.

All the signals from the AITC research (and from other surveys which preceded and followed it) are that private investors have not been put off by the volatile market conditions and are quite prepared to accept a degree of risk in order to achieve a superior rate of growth in their investment portfolio. It is for such investors that the following survey has been prepared.

This was a post-crash survey in the second half of 1988, and the trends are not likely to change dramatically in the foreseeable future. Prices change from day to day so those quoted here are given only as examples. You will need to obtain current prices once you make the decision to invest. However, the general observations do remain relevant. The investment trusts below are arranged under the main sectors of Smaller Companies and Special Features (as catalogued by the AITC) but are not otherwise presented in any particular order of size or success. Nor does the survey cover every possible trust in the field.

'Smaller company' investment trusts

Most of the investment trusts specialising in 'smaller companies' tend to have penny shares among their portfolios. Normally, such holdings seem to represent less than 5 per cent of the trust's total assets. A good example is the **Dundee & London Investment Trust** which reported £60 million under management. This trust normally has 5 per cent of its money in companies which can be classified as 'penny shares' (under 50p). Such shares carry a higher risk and 'investment selection takes this into account'. Performance has been in line with the market since October 1987.

The Smaller Companies International Trust managed by Edinburgh Fund Managers, also has £60 million under management. Here penny shares represented just under 2 per cent of the total portfolio valuation. The geographical breakdown of investments was UK 93 per cent, Japan 6 per cent and the USA 1 per cent. The share price of this trust fell sharply after the crash but recovered strongly throughout the first half of 1988. The managers claimed it had 'consistently out-performed the investment trust sector average'.

Shares priced at 50p or less comprised 1.5 per cent of the portfolio of the **St Andrew Trust** (£77 million under management by Martin Currie Investment Management). This trust looked for companies giving 'above average performance, both in terms of earnings and dividend growth'. The managers observed that 'the fact a share price is 10p rather than £10 seldom ensures outperformance over the medium to long term and is not a criterion for an investment'. Investment is in smaller companies, both at home and abroad. St Andrew Trust can claim to have outperformed its own investment trust sector over one, two or three years although its performance is not strictly comparable to others in the smaller companies field because of its international spread and the desire to pay 'consistently rising dividends'.

The **Kleinwort Development Fund** (£18 million of assets under management) invests in small companies, often those unquoted or traded on the USM. This trust was floated in June 1986 at £1.54 a share. The price was standing at £2.40 at the time of writing. The managers are Kleinwort Benson Development Capital Limited.

The **Kleinwort Smaller Companies Investment Trust** does not have any particular bias towards penny shares but roughly 10 per cent of the holding is in such equities. At the time of survey the trust was invested in around 120 small UK concerns with the aim of achieving 'above average performance'. The managers research specialist areas and companies which appear to have good management and products. Managed by Kleinwort Grieveson Investment Management, there was £26.5 million invested. AITC statistics show that the trust had fared as follows to mid-1988: one year 27.4

per cent down; two years 61 per cent increase; five years 249 per cent plus; ten years up 651 per cent.

There were no 'penny' holdings, on the other hand, in the **Moorgate Investment Trust** which reported £32 million under management. Here, the mix was rather different. Investments were made in smaller concerns, but sometimes larger companies were chosen where there appeared to be potential for growth through re-rating or takeover activity. Nine months after the crash, the share price was standing at 1 per cent above the October 1987 low. To mid-1988, there had been a compound growth rate of 31.4 per cent over five years and 27.8 per cent over ten.

Strata Investments offers the opportunity of investing in smaller companies on an international basis. The geographical spread at the time of survey was: UK 54 per cent; North America 19 per cent; Japan 18 per cent; Europe 9 per cent. Managed by Henderson Administration, funds under management exceeded £23 million. There was just one penny stock, representing 1.3 per cent of the UK portfolio. Strata Investments, launched in October 1985, traded at a premium at first, then moved to a discount in early 1987. Share price since the crash has been disappointing to the managers, though the underlying stocks have generally performed well.

TR Trustees Corporation (£301 million under management) is one of the largest trusts and pins its hopes for capital and income growth on smaller companies. The principal areas of investment are the UK, the US and Japan. Penny shares form a part of the portfolio. Early in the second half of 1988 the proportion of the total assets invested in penny shares was 1.33 per cent. (This ratio is related to the total assets of the fund and not just the UK investments.) The share price rose by 96.9 per cent in the three years to mid-July 1988. From the trough after the 1987 market down-turn the price had by that time risen 30.0 per cent to 127p.

Another trust investing in small companies worldwide is **F & C Smaller Companies**, managing assets of £90 million. The geographical division is: UK 50.8 per cent; North America 23.3 per cent; Japan 14.5 per cent; Europe 8.7 per cent; and South East Asia 2.7 per cent. Of these the penny share element was said to be 'minimal'. If you had invested £1000 in this trust in the spring of 1978 it would have been worth £8167 ten years later. The share price in mid-1988 was 20 per cent up on that at the time of the crash.

Gartmore Investments Limited manage two investment trusts which keep an eye on smaller companies. Their **London &**

Strathclyde Trust (£40.6 million under management) concentrates on smaller companies, emerging industries and unlisted investments. There are no penny stocks, by our definition, among them. The value of net assets had fallen by 22.5 per cent since the crash. The same company looks for capital growth through unquoted UK companies thought to have 'long-term potential for market listing or sale' in its **English & Caledonian** trust. Here assets under management totalled £11.3 million and the post-crash decline in net assets was 5.7 per cent.

'There is really no such thing as a penny share on the continent' said Ivory & Sime plc, managers of the **Continental Assets Trust**. Here the interest is in small companies and 'alternative markets' in continental Europe. 'Small' in this context means companies with a market capitalisation of up to the equivalent of £50 million. The 'alternative markets' covered include the French Second Market and the Dutch Parallel Market. Share price performance since the depressed post-crash conditions has been brisk with the price 29.7 per cent up between the end of 1987 and 31 July 1988.

Investors seeking both growth and a return on their money are wooed by the **Throgmorton Trust** (£351 million in assets under management). Investment is in smaller companies, principally in the UK and the aim is both 'capital appreciation and a worthwhile flow of dividends'. At the time of survey 10 per cent of the investments were 'pennies'. Total return on the share price over five years has been 309.9 per cent.

'Special features' investment trusts

About 10 per cent of the portfolio of the **Fleming Fledgeling Investment Trust** is in penny shares. The managers assert there have been 'some winners in this category' but stress that everything depends upon the individual company managements. Managed by the Robert Fleming group, there are assets under management here of £33 million. Capital appreciation is sought from small British and American companies, with the current emphasis on the former. By August 1988 the share price had improved 38 per cent since October 1987. The share price as of 30 June 1988 had increased by 94 per cent over three years and 113 per cent over five years.

'Emerging companies' at home and overseas are the interest of the **Fleming Mercantile Investment Trust** which dates from 1884. Assets under management exceed £360 million. Of the portfolio 5 per cent is in penny shares but the managers emphasise they have been selected because of their 'emerging' potential rather than simply because they are 'pennies'. Share price was 2.49 per cent up on November 1987 by August 1988. Over 10 years to early 1988 the share price had increased by 569 per cent. The rise over five years then was 123 per cent.

Very few penny shares figure in the portfolio of the **Fleming Enterprise Investment Trust** which has £66 million under management. Here the twin targets are British firms which have not yet achieved a Stock Exchange listing, and UK small companies. The share price has risen by 37 per cent since the crash. This is not far below the 40.2 per cent growth figure in the five years to 30 June 1988.

Consolidated Venture Trust is designed for the investor who believes there is scope in the 'special situations' sector, especially in the USA. The managers take a keen interest in 'small company reconstructions' across the Atlantic. An unquoted firm likely to come to market in three to four years' time is a typical target. Of the portfolio 3 per cent is devoted to penny shares. The share price, when the company was surveyed, had increased to 303p from the 281p level at which it stood after the crash. Assets under management exceed £30 million.

Growth through venture capital investment in the USA is also the objective of the **London American Ventures Trust**, formerly known as the London Trust plc. Registered as long ago as 1889, it has assets of £63 million, with management in the hands of Hambrecht & Quist Venture Partners and Ivory & Sime plc. There are no holdings of shares in UK companies. Most of the investments are in unlisted USA concerns with the proportion being 65 per cent unlisted and only 35 per cent listed. Eventually, perhaps during the trust's centenary year in 1989, it will rise to 100 per cent unlisted. This is because the typical target company these days tends to be unquoted. In some cases the trust is in 'turnaround' situations but here, as often as not, any quote is only marginal. The formula seems to work. In late October 1987, the price was 47p; at the end of the year it stood at 44p. The trust entered the second half of 1988 with the price well up at 56p.

There are not many penny shares in the property sector these days, thanks to out-performance of companies in recent years. There is, however, one trust which provides an entry into the 'junior' property sector, some of them still being in the 'penny' category. **TR Property Investment Trust** operates on a worldwide basis and when surveyed their portfolio showed about 4.5 per cent of the gross assets were invested in shares priced at the equiv-valent of 50p or less. The trust's experience has been that, in the buoyant property markets prevailing in Britain and other countries, such shares have generally performed impressively. More than £100 million is invested in the UK, with an emphasis on smaller property companies. Of this £12 million is in unquoted companies. The share price has risen by 170 per cent in five years. It fell to 72p during the crash but had recovered to 104p at time of writing. Assets under management exceed £168 million.

The **Value and Income Trust** has a novel approach. Its assets are divided equally between UK equities (including smaller companies, special situations and convertibles) and high yielding commercial property let to good tenants on long leases. The trust's managers say sternly they concentrate on good value and high yields 'and are not swayed by current fashions'. They had 'very few' penny shares in the portfolio when interviewed and felt that such shares only achieved relevance in over-heated markets such as those which prevailed before October 1987. The managers, Stewart Olim Limited, have £41 million under management. The share price has stood up reasonably well since the crash – it was 61p on 30 September 1987 and 54p in July of the following year. The managers assert this was due to their 'value' approach and their 'over-caution' before the down-turn in maintaining a high level of liquidity.

Situations where the managements may be tempted to arrange buy-outs are the special interest of **Candover Investments plc**. This trust says its principal activity is to 'identify, investigate, syndicate and invest in larger management buy-outs'. When surveyed 44 per cent of its investments were in unlisted companies, 28 per cent in listed, and the balance in cash. None of these investments were then regarded as being in the 'penny shares' category. Assets under management totalled £28 million. The unusual policy of finding situations where the management were likely to bid seems to have served Candover Investments well. The shares were listed in December 1984 at 160p. They reached a high point in the bull market of 420p at the end of July 1987 and stood at 250p by December of that year. At the time of survey the price was 397p.

If you are excited by the potential of USM companies then the **Throgmorton USM Trust** may be of interest. Here the aim is capital growth by investing chiefly in companies quoted on the Unlisted Securities Market. At least three-quarters of the trust's gross assets are in USM shares. Penny shares account for 8 per cent of the total assets which were valued at £32 million.

The same managers (Throgmorton Investment Management Services) direct the affairs of **Alva**, a trust which invests in private companies with 'good prospects of coming to the stock market'. Holdings of penny shares are said to be 'insignificant' at this stage. The share price here has recovered since the crash. It stood at 188p on 31 December 1987 and was 198p six months later. This is a small trust with £4.3 million under management.

Two trusts managed by old-established companies have special interest in management buy-out situations in Britain. They are the **F & C Enterprise Trust** (sometimes called Facet) and the **Murray Ventures**. Facet (£65 million managed) looks for unquoted companies internationally, but places an emphasis on management buy-outs to achieve long-term growth. All its penny shares were previously in the unquoted portfolio before going public. F & C state, 'We see no material difference between their performance and that of shares at higher levels.' Facet's share price recovered from 26 to 30p between December 1987 and mid-1988.

Murray Ventures is of similar size (£70 million) and invests in unquoted companies across a broad spectrum of industries with a particular emphasis on management buy-outs. There are both quoted and unquoted investments. At the time of the survey there were no penny shares in the portfolio. Surveying performance since the stock market downturn, one fair approach is to compare the change in the net assets of Murray Ventures with the change in the FT All Share Index. Between 30 September 1987 and 30 June 1988 the FT All Share Index fell by 20.3 per cent while the net asset value per Murray Ventures share fell by 9.9 per cent.

If you are interested in venture capital overseas, then there is the **London American Ventures Trust** (managed by Hambrecht & Quist with assets of £70 million) and the **Independent Investment Company** (Hambrecht & Quist with Ivory & Sime, managing £60 million). Neither had any penny shares in their portfolios at the time of the survey. The Independent Investment Company looks for new ventures on an international basis. Its share price stood at 48p after the crash but had recovered to 51p by the end of July 1988.

In the past year or so investment trusts have become increasingly available to small investors by means of monthly savings schemes. At the time of writing, it was possible to invest on a monthly basis in ten trusts with stakes in smaller companies and eight in the 'special features' category. The sums involved vary from company to company, but tend to be £20, £25 or £30 per month. The trusts involved are listed below:

Smaller Companies: Continental Assets; Dundee & London; English & International; F & C Smaller Companies; First Charlotte Assets; Fleming Fledgeling; Kleinwort Smaller Companies; St Andrew; TR Trustees Corporation; Throgmorton Trust.

Special Features: Alva; Drayton Consolidated; F & C Enterprise; Fleming Enterprise; Fleming Mercantile; Independent; Murray Ventures; TR Property.

8

THE RULES OF THE GAME

So, you have decided to play the penny share game. Your basic investment requirements have been met. You have acquired, or are buying your house. You have some 'sensible' investments and cash you can call upon from a bank or building society. You have adequate life assurance and insurance cover. Now you want to devote part of your portfolio to investments which carry an element of risk but also offer the prospect of higher than usual growth – and fun in the process. You have accepted the premise that investing in penny shares, or collective vehicles covering 'pennies' and smaller companies generally, is the best way of achieving these twin aims. All 'games' have their rules and here are a dozen for the penny share newcomer:

The rules

No matter how excited you may become about penny share opportunities, do not at any time borrow to buy. Get your priorities right and always keep some money available in a bank or building society to meet emergencies. Only hazard money you can afford (however reluctantly) to lose.

If you are going to become involved in investment you must be prepared to spend time learning about industry and commerce and keeping abreast of the stock market. This means investing, at least, in a serious daily newspaper, in one or more tip sheets, or personal finance publications, and in learning how to make use of the numerous forms of instant information now available.

- When you have selected a few investments in penny shares o smaller companies, *do* try to find out all you can about thos companies through reading their published statements an seeking the information to which a shareholder is entitled. B *do not* become totally obsessed with the companies of you choice and ignore the economy as a whole. You will not be abl to make proper decisions without taking account of currer developments in interest rates, inflation, the international valu of sterling, and so on.

- Adopt a firm investment policy and stick to it. Self-discipline all important. Fix in advance a percentage decline in the prid at which you will sell automatically. Base this, say, on the middl price and you will always be able to compare like with like. Wit penny shares you will have to fix a pretty high percentage fa (perhaps 50 per cent or thereabouts) to cover the wide dealir spreads.

- A similar policy has to be devised for taking a profit, but th can be operated more flexibly. Begin with a theoretical percen age price rise at which you should consider selling. If the pric continues to rise, then the percentage figure can be increase by a modest amount with each further jump. Should the pric then fall back, you sell at the latest revised percentage and thu ensure a sale ahead of your own initial calculations. If you ar fortunate enough to have a lively broker this formula can l applied automatically on your behalf. It is more likely thes days, however, that you will have to take action yourself or giv the necessary instructions to an intermediary.

- Some advisers urge you to sell half your holding if and when penny share doubles in price. In that way, you recover you original investment and place it elsewhere while the other ha of the holding stays to produce more growth and earning (This is a sensible approach, but it may involve a sizeable lo of potential profit.)

- Do not have 'favourites' among your shareholdings. Nev make excuses for an equity which has slumped considerably i value because you feel, somehow, that it is going to recove And do not become so fascinated by a rising share that yo neglect to sell at, or near, the optimum point. You buy to mak a profit. Fix a formula and apply it to all your holdings and t each sector.

- Accept that, as a small investor, you will not be able to mak gains to rival those of the entrepreneurs revitalising ailir companies, or the major investors in the market. Be prepare however, to act swiftly to benefit from their activities and to claim a healthy share of the profits they generate. Remember that someone always knows more than you do.

- Be cautious about acting on tips and gossip from people supposedly 'in the know'. The strong probability is that they know little of value. If they really have inside information, perhaps as employees of public companies or advisers to listed firms, they may come into the category of being 'insiders'. Acting on such privileged information for profit could put you in a difficult situation and perhaps even face you with a prosecution.

- The day of the week when you buy or sell can be important. The weekend produces a great deal of press comment and investors tend to read finance publications and tipsheets on Saturdays and Sundays. Many people issue buying orders on Mondays and Tuesdays and this can be a time to unload shares favourably. Thursdays and Fridays, especially near the end of a Stock Exchange account period, often see a great deal of selling. These days should generally be avoided, although sometimes there are bargains to be picked up if disappointed market professionals are unloading shares which failed to 'take off'.

- You will read numerous articles in the personal finance pages about taxation. Do not let the demands of the Inland Revenue influence you unduly. Unearned incomes are taxed far more sympathetically now than once they were and the current rates are far from onerous. Do not become obsessed by tax planning considerations – make the profit first! Do keep detailed records of all transactions for the day the tax man cometh.

- As you make investments, your name will become known to various marketing organisations selling financial products. Access to share registers can be obtained, quite properly, by people building up mailing lists. Such 'junk mail' annoys some people and you have the option nowadays of asking for your name to be removed from commercial lists. The more rational thing to do is to sift the grain from the chaff of the mailshots. Some of it may be of relevance and produce profits for you. Do not get involved in buying shares offered to you on the telephone. Such callers will, almost invariably, be unauthorised and the equities they are peddling of minimal, if any, value.

Making your purchase

You will be aware that nowadays there are a variety of channels through which shares can be purchased from stockbrokers and banks to telephone-based organisations and building societies. Purchases of unit trusts will be made through an intermediary, an in-house salesman, or by direct contact with the product company concerned. If you are going to employ the services of a stock-broker, you will need to understand the three main ways in which they work:

1. **Execution only** where the broker buys or sells for you in the market. You are charged a commission for all such services, but no advice is given.
2. **Discretionary service**. Here, the broker consults you about your investment objectives and asks about your tax position. Are you seeking capital growth or are you mainly in search of income? You then give him discretion to buy and sell on your behalf, while always keeping you informed. Each broking firm has its own idea of the minimum size of portfolio it will accept for such arrangements. Most talk nowadays of a portfolio of at least £20,000 but there are one or two small firms which will handle as little as £5000, while asserting it is 'scarcely economic' for them to do so.
3. **Portfolio advisory service**. Again, you agree your investment objectives first with the broker who then provides you with advice, information and recommendations. It is up to you to consider such proposals and to approve them before any action is taken. Fees for such attention vary from broker to broker.

The purchase and sale of shares is governed by a simple and straightforward procedure. Following an instruction to an inter-mediary to buy on your behalf, you are sent a contract note con-firming the deal. This is your temporary proof of ownership and must be kept for tax purposes. Your name is recorded in the share register of the company of your choice. It then sends you a share certificate which is your permanent proof of ownership. On selling, you give instructions to sell either 'at best' or above a minimum figure. Then you have to sign a transfer form which is sent, with the share certificate, to your intermediary. Your name is sub-sequently deleted from the share register in question.

Dealing in penny shares you will be involved with what the stock market now regards as delta shares. Under the new classifi-cation stocks and shares (listed and unlisted) are classified according to their marketability. Shares traded actively in large volumes are known as alpha stocks; the number of market makers registered to deal in these securities must be 10 or more. The criterion for beta stocks is that there must be a least six market makers. (In certain conditions, a stock where there are four or more market makers can be classified as a beta.) Gamma stocks must be supported by two market makers, each of which is prepared to quote indicative rather than firm prices. Delta stocks are difficult or unpopular shares that can only be traded by bargain-matching. Trading rules differ from stock to stock.

Unit trust investments have to be paid for immediately. With shares, on any of the stock market tiers, you get a little time to pay. The International Stock Exchange year is divided into account periods which normally comprise 10 working days, but may vary a little because of bank holidays. You have to pay before Settlement Day because that is when the broker settles up with market makers for all business done during the account period. In the ordinary course of business, Settlement Day falls six working days after the end of the account. You will always be given the precise date in the information printed on your contract.

Sources of information

In Chapter 9 you will find detailed information on the providers of instant information to the private investor. Most people, however, will be more familiar with the Stock Exchange prices as provided by the quality newspapers and, in particular, the *Financial Times*. This newspaper gives the widest press coverage of the markets but even the *Financial Times* does not cover all the shares traded on the International Stock Exchange. It is, however, essential reading for the investor. Even if you cannot keep up with it all the week, the comprehensive Saturday edition is excellent value for the penny share investor because it covers numerous equities traded in low volumes and not included in its weekday columns.

The *Financial Times* is also good value for its daily unit trust prices and for its Monday departure from routine by publishing the market capitalisation of each company quoted (valuable information for the small investor). Monday also gives you the last ex-dividend date (when the seller, not the buyer will benefit from the dividend) and the months in the year when dividends are normally paid. On other days, the *Financial Times* follows the pattern of such publications as *The Times*, *Daily Telegraph*, the *Guardian*, and the *Independent* in giving basic information for the investor on each company. Various columns cover the following:

- **High and low**. The highest and lowest prices at which the stock in question has been traded during the current calendar year.

- **The price**. The price, quoted in pence, is an approximation and normally the middle between the bid and offer prices.
- **Price movement**. This column in the tables shows how much the price has risen, or fallen, on the previous day's closing figure.
- **Dividends**. This entry discloses how much profit the company returned to its investors for each share they owned at the last distribution. When quoted 'net' it is the figure after deduction of tax.
- **Cover**. The ratio between a company's total profit and the amount of profit which it distributes to shareholders in the form of dividends. A dividend is, for example, 'twice covered' if the total value represents half the profits of the enterprise.
- **Gross yield** is the dividend, expressed as a percentage of the share price, and therefore an indication of how much a share is actually yielding in income terms. Thus, if a company pays a dividend of 10p per share, and the price is £1, then its gross yield is 10 per cent.
- **Price/earnings ratio** is the share price divided by the most recent year's earnings per share. For example, a company with a quoted price of £1 with earnings of 10p per share has a PE/ratio of 10:1.

Note that not all newspapers carry all the above entries in their tabular information. Nor are all quoted companies covered, even in the *Financial Times*. Companies normally have to pay to have their prices quoted and not all wish to bear this expense, or take the view that the market in their shares is not active enough to warrant daily exposure. A further point to note is that nowadays newspapers which offer readers telephone information services (see Chapter 3) often print alongside the company's information the code number which gives access to information on the price at any time.

There is thus more, and better, information available for the investor than at any time in the past. And, as we have seen, tipsheets providing 'buy' and 'sell' recommendations are obliged to carry out far more detailed research than hitherto. So there is no need for you to invest in ignorance, although you must always bear in mind the warning that prices can go down as well as up.

9
SERVICES YOU MAY FIND USEFUL

Investor protection

The two most useful addresses for the private investor are those of The Securities and Investments Board which supervises the activities of the various Self-Regulating Organisations (SROs) and of FIMBRA, one of those bodies, which is concerned with firms which offer investment advice and services to the public.

The SIB will answer enquiries, register complaints, and provide literature as below:

The Securities and Investments Board Limited
3 Royal Exchange Buildings
London EC3V 3NL;
Tel: 01–283 2474 (ask for the Information Officer)
       01–929 3652 (for Central Register enquiries)

Members of the public can check whether a firm is fully or interim authorised by SIB by telephoning its Central Register or by consulting page 301 of Prestel.

FIMBRA publishes various leaflets on its activities. These can be obtained by sending a stamped addressed envelope to:

FIMBRA
Hertsmere House
Marsh Wall
London E14 9RW
Tel: 01–929 2111

Stock Exchange

A good starting point for the private investor is the International Stock Exchange itself. The Publications Department at the Stock Exchange, Old Broad Street, London EC2. (Tel: 01–588 2355) will send you, free of charge, a booklet entitled *An Introduction to the Stock Market*. This is a simply written guide to the workings of the exchange and the buying and selling of shares. The Stock Exchange Publications Department also has numerous leaflets on aspects of investment. Individual ones are free; modest charges are made when more than one leaflet is required. The Wider Share Ownership Council has produced *The Private Investors Directory* (price £1) which lists stockbrokers all over the UK who are prepared to act for small investors.

Serious investors can subscribe to three official publications which are essential working tools for stockbrokers. *The Stock Exchange Weekly Official List* is published on Saturdays and available on Mondays. It lists all official notices and gives daily closing prices on all three markets. The price per issue is £6.50 (collected) or £7.50 (mailed). A quarterly subscription costs £70. *The Stock Exchange Official Yearbook* is published every January and gives comprehensive information on all companies listed and on members. This massive work costs £115 if collected and £121.20 when posted.

The Stock Exchange Investment List is a monthly publication which traces price movements in all securities in a small, handy format. A single copy costs £2.28 from the publishers:

Bishopsgate Press Limited
37 Union Street
London SE1 1SE
The annual subscription is £24.61.

Investors seeking more comprehensive information can subscribe to *The Hambro Company Guide*, published four times a year, at a subscription of £59.50. Publishers are:

Hemmington Scott Publishing Limited
Greenhill House
90–93 Cowcross Street
London EC1M 6BH

Stockbrokers

The reluctance of most stockbrokers to deal in penny shares (for a variety of reasons some good, some not) has been noted else-where in this book. The following dozen firms have confirmed to the author their willingness to deal in 'pennies' for private clients.

Hill Osborne & Company
Permanent House
Horsefair Street
Leicester LE1 5BU
Tel: 0533 29185

John Siddall & Son Limited
The Stock Exchange Buildings
Norfolk Street
Manchester M60 1DY
Tel: 061–832 7471

Hill Osborne & Company
Auburn House
8 Upper Piccadilly
Bradford BD1 3PA
Tel: 0274 728866

Stock Beech & Company
Bristol & West Buildings
Broad Quay
Bristol BS1 4DD
Tel: 0272 260051

R N McKean & Company
11 Grove Place
Bedford
MK40 3JJ
Tel: 0234 51131

Stock Beech & Company
Wanford Court
Throgmorton Street
London EC2N 2AY
Tel: 01–638 8471

National Investment Group
Penniless Porch
Market Place
Wells,
Somerset

Stock Beech & Company
75 Edmund Street
Birmingham
B3 3HL
Tel: 021–236 5151

National Investment Group
Jacey House
The Landsdowne
Bournemouth
BH1 2PP

R L Stott & Company (IOM) Limited
Exchange House
Athol Street
Douglas
Isle of Man
Tel: 0624 73701

Rensburg
Silk House Court
Tithe Barn Street
Liverpool L2 2NH
Tel: 051–227 2030

Torrie & Company
37 Frederick Street
Edinburgh
EH2 1EP

Independent financial advice

The Campaign for Independent Financial Advice (CAMIFA) dis-tributes a free booklet on the implications of the Financial Services

Act and the new protection which it should provide for consumers.

Copies can be obtained by telephoning 01–200 3000. Callers are also given a list of all the independent financial advisers in their area.

Share price information services

For details of British Telecom's Citycall telephone-based services write to:

Citycall
Freepost
Newbury RG13 1BR
(No stamp required)

Information on the Teleshare system of providing share information by telephone can be obtained from:

Teleshare Customer Liaison Department
Telephone Information Services Limited
Dewhurst House
24 West Smithfield
London EC1A 9DL
Tel: 01–489 1946

Six national newspapers offer information services by telephone. The relevant telephone numbers are:

Financial Times Cityline 0898–123 456
The Times Stockwatch 0898–141 141
The Daily Telegraph Teleshare Service 0898–500 556
The Observer Business Line 0898–123 200
The Guardian Sharecall 0898–345 350
The Independent Index 0898–123 333

Shoppers who know the Debenham Group of retail stores can use a similar service known as Debenhams Teleshare. (Telephone 0898–500 505.) There is also a Telegrade card for customers who deal by telephone.

The Prestel CitiService requires an existing telephone and an adapted television or microcomputer, or a dedicated Prestel set. Details from:

ICV Information Systems Limited
Woodsted House
72 Chertsey Road
Woking GU21 5BJ

Pont Advantage is a financial information service with an annual subscription of £99 for non-professional users. It is available over the Fastrak or Mercury national networks using a personal computer or videotext terminal (similar to Prestel). The address is:

Pont Advantage
6 City Road
London EC1Y 2AA
Tel: 01–247 8151

Share dealing by telephone

Sharelink Limited, a subsidiary of British Telecom, is a seven-days-a-week share dealing service by telephone. It is managed by the stockbroking firm of Albert E. Sharp & Company:

Sharelink
Post Office Box 1063
Birmingham B3 3ET
Tel: 021–200 2242

Fidelity offer a cost efficient service for the serious private investor – but it is not for the person who seeks advice or plans to trade only a few times in a year. The service operates from 8 am until 6 pm, Monday to Friday:

Fidelity Portfolio Services Limited
Oakhill House
Hildenborough
Tonbridge
Kent TN11 9DZ
Tel: 0800–800 700

Penny share publications

The Penny Share Guide is available on an annual subscription of £59.50. In their promotional activities, however, the publishers often offer a reduced subscription of £39.50 for the first year only. Ask about that if you are interested in becoming a subscriber. Write to:

The Penny Share Guide Limited
FREEPOST (no stamp required)
4 Abbots Place
London NW6 1YP
Tel: 01–625 6300

Linked with the Guide is a Penny Share Telephone Service, updated twice a week, which gives topical information on prices and deals and suggests investment opportunities. The charge is the same as the other telephone service (38p per minute in the peak period, 25p at off-peak times) and the number is: 0898–345 301.

Penny Share Focus has the same annual subscription as the Guide (£59.50) and can similarly be obtained at a reduction of £20 for the first year. The address here is:

Penny Share Focus
11 Blomfield Street
London EC2M 7AY

The New Issue Share Guide, covering market newcomers, is published from the same address as the *Penny Share Guide*. Subscription rate is £49.50 for the first year, then £69.50 thereafter. Useful information on new enterprises can be found in *Venture Opinion*, again published from 4 Abbotts Place, where the respective subscription rates are £39.50 and £59.50.

Business Expansion Scheme sponsors

If you are interested in investing in companies which are both new and small then it makes sense to get on the mailing lists of some of the top firms which sponsor BES issues. Here are some companies to which you might write:

Johnson Fry plc
Dorland House
20 Regent Street
London SW1
Tel: 01–439 0924 and 01–499 5066

Chancery Corporate Services
14 Fitzhardinge Street
Manchester Square
London W1H 9PL
Tel: 01–486 7171

Guidehouse Limited
Vestry House
Greyfriars Passage
Newgate Street
London EC1 7BA
Tel: 01–606 6321

Capital Ventures Limited
37 London Road
Cheltenham
Gloucestershire
Tel: 0242–584390

Centreway Development Capital Limited
1 Waterloo Street
Birmingham B2 5PG
Tel: 021–643 3941

Low price BES shares
The publications below carry news of BES issues, some of which are priced attractively low. The majority of such issues these days, however, tend to be out of the penny share category:

John Spiers
BESt Investment (available by subscription at £130 per annum)
4 New Bridge Street
London EC4V 6AA
Tel: 01–353 0301

or

Anthony Yadgaroff
Best BES (available by subscription at £97.50 per annum)
60 St James's Street
London SW1A 1LE
Tel: 01–409 1111

Investment Trusts

A variety of useful information can be obtained from publications published or sponsored by The Association of Investment Trust Companies (AITC) which has been established for more than half a century. It has 161 investment trusts as members, all listed on the International Stock Exchange.

How To Make It is published annually by Woodhead-Faulkner of Cambridge in association with the AITC. It is a substantial paperback, priced at £5.95. Investment trusts are described in detail in the first part of the book. Then follows a directory giving facts and figures on each trust, together with a useful historical record.

The AITC also publishes with Woodhead-Faulkner the *Investment Trust Directory*, priced at £25. There is a free pack from the AITC which includes a leaflet *Explaining Investment Trusts*. The address is:

The Association of Investment Trust Companies, Park House (Sixth Floor), 16 Finsbury Circus, London EC2M 7JJ. Tel: 01-588 5347.

The most recent performance figures are contained in the AITC's Monthly Information Service. This provides comprehensive performance data on investment trusts and costs £20 for an annual subscription. Intermediaries, in addition, have had access since mid-1988 to an Investment Trust Index. Clients can always ask for the figures contained in that index, circulated exclusively to professional advisers.

Most managers of investment trusts offer savings schemes nowadays, under which you can invest sums of £20, £25, or £30 each month. The AITC will supply the names and addresses of such companies.

Unit trusts

The Unit Trust Association embraces most of the management groups (153 at time of writing) which handle the country's 1,200-plus unit trusts. Its own membership is in excess of 130 management groups. The UTA is a useful source of information for both new investors and those who wish to keep abreast of developments in the movement.

There are three publications which the UTA will send you free of charge. *A Simple Guide to Unit Trusts* runs to 28 pages in A5 format and is bang up to date, with all the necessary information on the unit trust industry in the wake of the Financial Services Act.

Everything You Need to Know About Unit Trusts is a well established 40-page A4 publication which lists all the management groups and their funds. It is particularly useful in that it gives minimum investment figures, management charges, and other basic information.

The third free UTA booklet is the *Unit Trust Association Annual Review* which is essentially an annual report. Its 12 pages are devoted to essentially statistical information in the manner of a public company's annual report. You can check the full membership of the UTA in the review.

For those who prefer instruction on video, the UTA has a 14-minute production called 'In At The Shallow End' which is a simple introduction to the world of unit trusts. This costs £5 to hire or £25 to buy.

If you are prepared to invest £10 in a more substantial publication, there is *Unit Trusts and the Financial Services Act*, published jointly with Touche Ross Management Consultants. This new publication surveys the changes brought about in the unit trust industry by the Financial Services Act and is a general reference to the new regime. The address to write to is:

Unit Trust Association
65 Kingsway
London WC2B 6TD
Tel: 01–831 0898

GLOSSARY

Finally, as you 'dip your toes' in the vast investment sea, the following glossary may be of value. The entries have been verified by the Unit Trust Association, the Association of Investment Trust Companies and the International Stock Exchange. This is by no means a comprehensive glossary, nor does it repeat all the descriptions of various institutions, products and services defined in detail elsewhere in this book.

Account. The principal division of the International Stock Exchange calendar. Normally an account runs for two weeks (10 working days).

Account day. The day on which all bargains done during an account are settled. Usually the second Monday following the end of the account.

Accumulation units. All income earned on investments is reinvested automatically in a unit trust. Accumulation units, therefore, enable investors to plough new money regularly into a unit trust without having to pay a further initial management charge.

After hours dealing. Dealings done after the end of the Stock Exchange's mandatory quote period, 9.00 am to 5.00 pm.

Agency broker. A broker who acts purely in a single capacity as an agent between the buyer and the seller and charges a commission for the service. Agency brokers do not act as market makers.

Annual General Meeting. Shareholders are given the opportunity once a year to question directors of the company in which they are invested and to go over the results of the previous year's trading.

They must be advised of such a meeting at least 21 days in advance and be sent the company's Report and Accounts. If the company wishes to make a major acquisition or disposal, or alter the capital structure, it calls an **Extraordinary General Meeting**.

Annual Report. This is an independently audited report which must be produced by all publicly quoted companies, and sent to their shareholders following the completion of each financial year. It records the year's trading results and the company's financial position at the year-end.

Application form. When a company offers shares to the public the official application form must be used to apply for them. This form is printed in the prospectus and in a national newspaper.

Approved investment trust. An investment trust which satisfies the requirements of Section 359 of the Income and Corporation Taxes Act 1970, as amended, and is therefore exempt from having to pay tax on the capital gains it realises from sales of the investments within its own portfolio.

Arbitrage. Buying securities in one country or currency and selling in another. Also now used to describe the practice of taking strategic stakes in companies involved, or likely to be involved, in a takeover bid.

Associated Member. A member of the International Stock Exchange in his own right who is not a partner or director of his member firm.

Association of Investment Trust Companies. Popularly known as the AITC, this association was founded in 1932 as the collective voice for UK investment trusts. It provides information direct to the investing public as well as looking after the interests of members and their shareholders.

Authorised share capital. Effectively, this figure is the ceiling for the amount of capital which a company can raise. It is usually far higher than the amount injected into the company and known as paid-up capital.

Authorised unit trust. A unit trust which has been approved by the Securities and Investments Board under the Financial Services Act 1986. Only authorised unit trusts can advertise and be offered for sale to the public.

B Shares. These are shares introduced in the 1960s by some investment trusts as a method of giving the shareholder a choice between income and capital return. The 'B' shareholder receives no dividends. Instead, he or she gets a regular scrip issue of 'B' shares based upon both the dividend paid on, and the value of, each ordinary share.

Bargain. Any Exchange transaction. No 'special price' is implied, contrary to the normal meaning of the word.

Bear. A pessimist, one who has sold a security in the hope of buying it back at a lower price. A bear market is one in which bears would prosper, that is, a falling market.

Bearer stocks/shares. Securities for which no register of ownership is kept by the company. A bearer certificate has an intrinsic value. Dividends are not received automatically from the company, but must be claimed by removing and returning 'coupons' attached to the certificate.

Bed and breakfast. Selling shares one day and buying them back the next, for tax purposes at the end of a financial year.

Beneficial owner. The ultimate owner of a security, regardless of the name in which it is registered.

Bid. 1. To indicate how much you are prepared to pay for shares. 2. An approach made by one company wishing to purchase the entire share capital of another company.

Big Bang. 27 October 1986, when the International Stock Exchange's new regulations took effect.

Blue chip. A term for the most highly regarded industrial shares. Originally an American term, derived from the colour of the highest value poker chip.

Broker/Dealer. An International Stock Exchange member firm which provides advice and dealing services to the public.

Bull. An optimist, one who has bought a security in the hope of selling it at a higher price. A bull market is therefore one in which bulls would prosper, that is, a rising market.

Business Expansion Scheme. A government scheme allowing investors to put money into unlisted companies with the benefit of tax relief.

Call. The amount due to be paid to a company by the purchaser of new or partly paid shares.

Call option. The right to buy stock or shares at an agreed price on a future date.

Capitalisation issue. The process whereby money from a company's reserves is converted into issued capital, which is then distributed to shareholders as new shares, in proportion to their original holdings. Also colloquially known as a bonus or scrip issue.

Chinese wall. Part of the jargon which has developed since Big Bang. The term is used to describe the internal walls which are designed to protect confidential information being passed improperly between departments within a financial organisation.

Closed-end fund. A medium, such as a UK investment trust, with a fixed capital structure. Variations in demand for the shares of the fund are reflected in movements in their market prices and not by an expansion or contraction in their supply.

Commission. The fee that a Member of the International Stock Exchange may charge clients for dealing on their behalf.

Compensation fund. The fund maintained by the International Stock Exchange to recompense investors should a member firm fail to meet its obligations and be 'hammered' (liquidated).

Concert party. A situation where there is an agreement to co-operate actively to acquire control of a company through planned purchases of shares in that company.

Consideration. The money value of an Exchange transaction (number of shares multiplied by the price) before adding commission, stamp duty, VAT, time of deal etc.

Contract note. On the same day as a bargain takes place a member firm must send to the client a contract note detailing the transaction, to include full title of the stock, price, consideration, stamp duty (if applicable) etc.

Convertible loan stock. Fixed interest loans which may be converted into ordinary shares at a future date. The terms of conversion are fixed at the date of the issue of the loan. The intention is to give the investor a yield higher than that of the company's ordinary shares at the date the convertible is issued, together with an opportunity of benefiting from the company's capital growth.

Coupon. 1. On bearer stocks, the detachable part of the certificate exchangeable for dividends. 2. Denotes the rate of interest on a fixed interest security – a 10 per cent coupon pays interest of 10 per cent per year.

Cover. The amount of money a company has available for distribution as dividend, divided by the amount actually paid gives the number of times that the dividend is covered.

Cum. Latin for 'with' used in the abbreviations Cum Cap, Cum Div, Cum Rights etc to indicate that the buyer is entitled to participate in the forthcoming capitalisation dividend or rights issue.

Debenture. A loan raised by a company, paying a fixed rate of interest and secured on the assets of the company.

Designated accounts. In the case of unit trusts, these are units purchased for a child but registered in the name of a parent or a guardian and 'designated' with the child's initials.

Dictum meum pactum. 'My word is my bond.' This is the proud motto of the International Stock Exchange where massive transactions are concluded with only verbal agreements.

Diluted net asset value. A method of calculating the net asset value of a company that has outstanding convertible loan stocks, warrants or options. Such a calculation assumes that the holders have exercised their right to convert or subscribe, thus increasing the number of shares among which the assets are divided.

Discount. This term is used when a market price of a newly issued security is lower than the issue price. If it is higher, the difference is called the premium.

Discounted. The City uses this word to indicate that some expected future event has already been allowed for in the current price.

Distribution period. The period during which income earned by a unit trust is accumulated before it is paid out to investors.

Dividend. That part of a company's post-tax profits distributed to shareholders, usually expressed in pence per share.

Equalisation. A refund of a small part of the initial investment which unit trust investors receive with their first income distribution. Income which has been earned by a trust since it last made a distribution is included in the offer price of units bought during that distribution period. The equalisation payment represents the amount of income which has accrued between the time of the last distribution and the time new investors bought their units. The payment is not subject to income tax.

Equity. The risk-sharing part of a company's capital, usually referred to as ordinary shares or preference shares.

Ex. Without. The opposite of Cum, and used to indicate that the buyer is not entitled to participate in whatever forthcoming event is specified. Ex Cap, Ex Dividend, Ex Rights, etc.

Exempt trust. Unit trusts only open for investments from charities and pension funds. These tax-exempt bodies are not liable to either UK income or capital gains tax.

Final dividend. The dividend paid by a company at the end of its financial year, recommended by the directors, but authorised by shareholders at the company's Annual General Meeting.

Fixed interest. Loans issued by a company, the Government (gilts or gilt-edged) or local authority, where the amount of interest to be paid each year is set on issue. Usually the date of repayment is also included in the title.

Flotation. The occasion on which a company's shares are offered on the market for the first time.

Franked income. Ordinary and preference dividends, plus the associated tax credits, paid by UK companies when received by other UK companies which are liable to corporation tax on their profits. As these distributions come from profits that have already been subject to tax in Britain, they are not liable to a further corporation tax charge.

FT Index. Refers to the Financial Times Industrial Ordinary Share Index, also known as the '30 Share Index'. This started in 1935 at 100, and is based on the prices of 30 leading industrial and commercial shares. They are chosen to be representative of British Industry, rather than of the Exchange. Government stocks, banks and insurance companies are not included. Calculated hourly during the day with a 'closing index' at 5.00 pm.

FT–SE 100 Share Index. Popularly known as 'Footsie', is an index of 100 leading UK shares listed on the International Stock Exchange and provides a minute by minute picture of how share prices are moving. It started in January 1984 with the base number of 1000. Also forms the basis of a contract in the Exchange's Traded Options Market.

Fully paid. Applied to new issues, when the total amount payable in relation to the new shares has been paid to the company.

Gearing. The proportional relationship between debt capital on the one hand and equity capital on the other.

Gilts or gilt-edged. Loans issued on behalf of the Government to fund its spending. **Longs**: those without a redemption date within 15 years. **Mediums**: those with a redemption date between 7 and 15 years. **Shorts**: those with a redemption date within 7 years.

Gross. Before deduction of tax.

Grossing-up. Calculating the amount that would be required, in the case of an investment subject to tax, to equal the income from an investment not subject to tax.

Hammering. Announcement of the failure of a member firm of the International Stock Exchange.

Income units. Unit trust investors with such units receive regular income payments from their unit holding. The payments are usually made twice a year, though a few unit trusts distribute income each quarter or month.

Index linked gilt. A gilt whose interest and capital change in line with the Retail Price Index.

Interim dividend. A dividend declared part way through a company's financial year, authorised solely by the directors.

Introduction. A method of bringing a company to the market. No new securities are issued. Allowed where shares issued are of such an amount and so widely held that their marketability when listed can be assured.

Investment trust. A company whose sole business consists of buying, selling and holding shares. Such a trust, when described as 'independent', is a company which employs its own staff, maintains its own in-house resources, and does not employ an outside firm for administrative or investment management services.

Issuing house. An organisation, usually a merchant bank, which arranges the details of an issue of stocks or shares, and the necessary compliance with the International Stock Exchange regulations in connection with its listing.

Letter of renunciation. Form attached to an allotment letter which is filled in should the original holder wish to pass his entitlement to someone else.

Limit. A restriction set on an order to buy or sell, specifying the minimum selling or maximum buying price.

Limited life trusts. These are companies with articles of association that require a resolution to wind up the company which must be put to shareholders at regular intervals, eg annually, or every five years. In a few cases, the articles require the shareholders to vote in favour of the resolution after a set term.

Liquidation. The process whereby a company's assets are realised, creditors are repaid, if possible, and the shareholders receive any remaining surplus according to their rights and priorities as stated in the articles of association.

Liquidity. In the case of unit trusts, this term refers to that part of a trust which is held in cash, not shares. The period during which a unit trust can hold cash before investing is strictly limited.

Listed company. A company that has obtained permission for its shares to be admitted to the International Stock Exchange's official list.

Listing particulars. The details a company must publish about itself and any securities it issues before these can be listed on any stock exchange in the European Community.

Loan stock. Stock bearing a fixed rate of interest. Unlike a debenture, loan stocks may be unsecured.

Management charge. The cost of running a unit, or an investment, trust charged annually by the managers. With unit trusts, there is also an initial charge of a typical 5 per cent to 6 per cent.

Market-maker. An Exchange member firm which is obliged to buy and sell securities, in which it is registered as a principal, at all times.

Member firm. A trading firm of the International Stock Exchange, may act as an agency broker on behalf of clients or as a market-maker.

Middle price. The price half-way between the two prices shown in the International Stock Exchange's Daily Official List under 'Quotation', or the average of both buying and selling prices offered by the market-makers. The prices found in newspapers are normally their estimate of the middle price.

Net asset value. The value of a company after all debts have been paid, expressed in pence per share.

New issue. The offer to the public, via a prospectus, of shares or loan capital in a company. In the case of share capital, this may take the form of as yet unissued shares or of issued shares made available by existing shareholders (usually to enable an unlisted company to acquire a listing).

Nil paid. A new issue of shares, usually as the result of a rights issue, on which no payment to the company has yet been made.

Nominee name. Name in which a security is registered that does not indicate who the beneficial owner is.

Offer. To indicate that you are prepared to sell shares at a particular price.

Offer for sale. A method of bringing a company to the market. The public can apply for shares directly at a fixed price. In general a prospectus must be printed in two national newspapers.

Official list. 1. The major of the Exchange's three markets for UK shares. 2. The International Stock Exchange's Daily Official List is the list of official prices published each day.

Offshore fund. A fund established outside the UK. Such funds are often run on unit trust lines, by UK investment management groups, and may accept money from UK investors.

Open-ended fund. A fund whose capital can usually be increased or decreased by managers without the approval of existing investors. Unit trusts are the best examples of such funds.

Option. The right (but not the obligation) to buy or sell a share at a set price within a set period.

Ordinary shares. The most common form of share. Holders receive dividends which vary in amount in accordance with the profitability of the company and recommendations of the directors. The holders of the ordinary shares are the owners of the company.

Par. The nominal value of a security (always taken as £100 in fixed interest stocks). By British and Irish company law, a company must set a par value on its ordinary shares. In some countries shares can have 'no par value' (abbreviated to NPV).

Placing. 1. A privately arranged transaction in which shares are bought for a price agreed by buyer and seller. 2. A means by which companies may float their securities on the stock market.

Portfolio. The list of securities owned by an individual or financial institution.

Pound/Cost averaging. The effect of investing a fixed sum of money regularly in a unit trust. The average price paid for units is lower than the average unit price over the savings period because the regular investment buys more units when the price is low, and fewer when it is high.

Preference shares. These are normally fixed-income shares, whose holders have the right to receive dividends before ordinary shareholders but after debenture and loan stock holders have received their interest.

Preferential form. The International Stock Exchange allows companies offering shares to the public to set aside up to 10 per cent of the issue for applications from employees and, where a parent company is floating off a subsidiary, shareholders of the parent company. Separate application forms, usually pink in colour (hence the nickname pink forms), are used for this.

Premium. If the market price of a new security is higher than the issue price, the difference is the premium. If it is lower, the difference is called the discount.

Price/Earnings ratio. The current share price divided by the last published earnings (expressed as pence per share). It is used as a measure of whether a share should be considered 'expensive'. Thus a share selling at 50p with a P/E ratio of 10 would be considered dearer than one selling at 100p with a P/E ratio of 5.

Probate price. The price used to assess the value of shares for inheritance tax purposes. Calculated on the 'quarter up' principle. That is, instead of taking the middle price in the Official List, the difference between the two prices given under 'quotation' is divided by four, and this amount added to the lower one.

Prospectus. Document giving the details that a company is required to make public, to support a new issue of shares.

Proxy. A person empowered by a shareholder to vote on his or her behalf at company meetings.

Put option. The right to sell stock at an agreed price on a future date.

Qualified accounts. Auditors give a warning light to investors when they 'qualify' a company's accounts, ie they cannot say they represent a totally true and fair view of the company's situation.

Redemption date. The date on which a security, (usually a fixed interest stock), is due to be repaid by the issuer at its full face value. The year is included in the title of the security; the actual redemption date being that on which the last interest is due to be paid.

Renounceable documents. Temporary evidence of ownership, of which there are four main types. When a company offers shares to the public, it sends an **allotment letter** to the successful applicants; if it has a rights issue, it sends a **provisional allotment letter** to its shareholders, or in the case of a capitalisation issue, a **renounceable certificate**. All of these are in effect bearer securities, and are valuable. Each includes full instructions on what the holder should do if he or she wishes to have the newly issued shares registered or wishes to renounce them in favour of somebody else. This facility applies for a strictly limited time.

Rights issue. When a company, whose shares are already listed, makes a new issue for cash to existing shareholders, in proportion to their holdings, this is usually made at a preferential price.

SEAQ. The Stock Exchange Automated Quotation system for UK securities. It is continuously updated computer database containing quotations and trade reports in UK securities. SEAQ is the official information source for trading UK securities.

SEAQ international. The Exchange's electronic screen system for non-UK equities displaying quotes from competing market-makers on composite pages.

Securities. The general name for all stocks and shares of all types. In common usage, stocks are fixed interest securities and shares are the rest, though strictly speaking, the distinction is that stocks are denominated in money terms. For example, ICI does not have any ordinary shares at all: its equity capital is in fact divided into units of ordinary stock, transferable in multiples of £1, but the difference between this and ordinary shares of £1 each is academic.

Share exchange schemes. These are plans which allow investors who own shares to exchange them usually on favourable terms, for units in a unit trust.

Split capital trust. This is an investment trust with a limited life, the equity capital of which is divided into income shares and capital shares.

Spread. The difference between the offer (buying) and bid (selling) unit price.

Stag. One who applies for a new issue in the hope of being able to sell the shares allotted to him or her at a profit as soon as dealing starts.

Stamp duty. A UK tax levied on the purchase of shares.

Talisman. The International Stock Exchange's computerised settlement system.

Tap stocks. Government stocks which the Government Broker (since Big Bang an official of the Bank of England) will supply at a given price. The price chosen provides a means of influencing interest rates in general.

Tax credit. A tax voucher showing the amount of income tax that a unit trust has paid on an investor's income. If that investor is not a taxpayer, the amount claimed can be repaid. Higher rate taxpayers will have a further amount to pay.

Tender offer. In an offer by tender, buyers of shares specify the price at which they are willing to buy.

Third Market. The Exchange's market for small companies, open for those who do not qualify for the Unlisted Securities Market (USM) or as a listed company.

Topic. The International Stock Exchange's own videotext terminal network. Used for disseminating, among much other information, SEAQ and SEAQ International.

Traded options. Transferable options with the right to buy and sell a standardised amount of a security at a set price within a set period.

Transfer. The form signed by the seller of a security authorising the company to remove his or her name from the register, and substitute that of the buyer.

Trust deed. The legal document which sets out how a unit trust shall be run. The trust deed is a unit trust's written constitution.

Trustee. Financial institutions like banks and insurance companies which hold a unit trust's securities and cash on behalf of investors, and generally watch over investors' interests.

Trustee status. Used with reference to ordinary shares of those companies which meet the requirements of 'wider range' investments as defined by the Trustee Investments Act 1961. Briefly, the company is UK registered, has paid-up capital of at least £1 million, and has paid a dividend for at least the last five years.

Underwriting. An arrangement by which a company is guaranteed that an issue of shares will raise a given amount of cash because the underwriters, for small commission, undertake to subscribe for any of the issue not taken up by the public.

Unfranked income. This is income subject to British Corporation Tax and includes interest from debenture and loan stocks, bank deposits, underwriting commissions and foreign earnings.

Unit trust. A portfolio of holdings in various companies, divided into units and managed by professionals.

Unit Trust Association. The UTA speaks for the unit trust industry and provides information to investors. Its members manage more than 95 per cent of the money invested in unit trusts.

Unlisted Securities Market (USM). The Exchange's market for medium-sized companies who do not qualify for, or do not wish, a full listing.

Unlisted security. One which has not been admitted to the Official List. Usually the issuer will be an unlisted company, but not always. It is not uncommon for a company to apply for its ordinary shares to be listed but not its loan stocks, or vice versa.

Warrant. A special kind of option, given by a company to holders of a particular security, giving them the right to subscribe for future issues, either of the same kind or some other security.

Withdrawal plans. Schemes to provide unit trust investors with regular or additional income. Income received from the trust's earnings is topped up by selling some of the investor's units on a regular basis.

Yield. The annual return on your money, based on the current price of the security, on the assumption that the next dividend paid will be the same as the last one. *Flat yield* is the income on a fixed interest stock, ignoring any capital gain that may be made if the stock is due to be redeemed at par at some future date. *Redemption yield* is the same, but allowing for the expected capital gain.

Zero coupon stock. This is loan stock which provides no annual interest to the investor. Instead, he or she receives stock priced considerably lower than the nominal value.

PERSONAL FINANCE TITLES FROM KOGAN PAGE

Blackstone Franks Good Investment Guide, The, David Franks, **1987**
Blackstone Franks Guide to Living in Spain, **1988**
Blackstone Franks Guide to Perks from Shares, **1988**
Buying and Selling a House or Flat, Howard and Jackie Green, **1988**
Cashwise: How to Achieve More from a Fixed Income, Frank Birkin, **1987**
Easing into Retirement, Keith Hughes, **1987**
How to Write a Will and Gain Probate, Marlene Garsia, **1989**
Living and Retiring Abroad, 3rd edn, Michael Furnell, **1989**
Managing Your Money, Anthea Masey, **1988**
Personal Pensions: The Choice is Yours, Norman Toulson, **1987**

Index

INDEX